Edward Jewitt Wheeler

Prohibition:

The principle, the policy and the party : a dispassionate study of the arguments for and against prohibitory law, and the reasons governing the political action of its advocates. Fifth Edition

Edward Jewitt Wheeler

Prohibition:
The principle, the policy and the party : a dispassionate study of the arguments for and against prohibitory law, and the reasons governing the political action of its advocates. Fifth Edition

ISBN/EAN: 9783337810887

Printed in Europe, USA, Canada, Australia, Japan

Cover: Foto ©ninafisch / pixelio.de

More available books at **www.hansebooks.com**

PROHIBITION:

THE PRINCIPLE, THE POLICY AND THE PARTY.

A DISPASSIONATE STUDY OF THE ARGUMENTS FOR AND AGAINST PROHIBITORY LAW, AND THE REASONS GOVERNING THE POLITICAL ACTION OF ITS ADVOCATES.

By E. J. WHEELER.

FIFTH EDITION.

"Unsettled questions have no mercy on the peace of nations."
—GARFIELD.

New York
FUNK & WAGNALLS COMPANY
LONDON AND TORONTO
1894

CONTENTS.

	Page.
PART I. THE PRINCIPLE.	1
1. THE LEGAL PHASE OF THE SUBJECT.	3
2. TWO VIEWS OF THE PROVINCE OF GOVERNMENT.	7
3. JOHN STUART MILL AND HERBERT SPENCER.	10
4. THE QUESTION OF PERSONAL LIBERTY	21
5. THE SIN PER SE.	27
6. THE CONTROVERSY OVER BIBLE WINES.	30
7. THE PHYSIOLOGICAL EFFECTS OF ALCOHOL.	39
8. DRINK AND CRIME.	49
9. DRINK AND DEATH.	57
10. THE ECONOMICAL EVILS OF DRINK.	67
11. POLITICAL EVILS DUE TO THE SALOON	76
12. THE PLEASURE OF DRINK.	88
13. RECAPITULATION.	92
PART II. THE POLICY.	94
1. THE INQUIRY INSTITUTED BY THE CANADIAN PARLIAMENT.	97
2. THE RESULT IN MAINE.	108
3. THE RESULT IN VERMONT.	121
4. THE RESULT IN KANSAS.	124

CONTENTS.

5. THE RESULT IN IOWA. 129
6. THE RESULT IN RHODE ISLAND. . 133
7. THE ATTITUDE OF THE LIQUOR DEALERS. 135
8. LEGAL AND MORAL RESULTS OF PROHIBITION. 138
9. THE DEMAND FOR NATIONAL PROHIBITION. 148

PART III. THE PARTY. 157
1. CAN THE REFORM BE ACCOMPLISHED THROUGH EITHER OLD PARTY? . . 163
2. THE BALANCE OF POWER PLAN . . 171
3. THE NON-PARTISAN PLAN OF UNION . 175
4. THE OBJECTIONS TO A NEW PARTY . 183
5. IS PUBLIC SENTIMENT READY? . . 190
6. OTHER ISSUES OF THE DAY . . . 195

APPENDIX 207

PART I. THE PRINCIPLE.

IS PROHIBITION IN ACCORD WITH WISE PRINCIPLES OF STATESMANSHIP?

" No legislation founded on unsound principles can accomplish a permanent good, whatever be the present seeming."—PREFACE TO BISHOP'S STATUTORY CRIMES.

"MEN are four," says an Arabic proverb:

"He who knows not, and knows not he knows not. He is a fool; shun him.

"He who knows not, and knows he knows not. He is simple; teach him.

"He who knows, and knows not he knows. He is asleep; wake him.

"He who knows, and knows that he knows. He is wise; follow him."

The only difficulty with this, as with so many other wise deliverances, lies in its application. For it frequently happens that the man who knows not that he knows not, and the man who knows that he knows, manifest the same characteristics, being equally positive and equally sincere. If emphasis in assertion is to be sole guide in deciding the righteousness of a cause, we shall be forced generally to conclude that each side is right.

Certainly this would be the case in the discussion of Prohibition, which has been characterized on both sides with much warmth of feeling and a consequent warmth of utterance. It has been made a theme of heated controversy in the realm of science, of philosophy, and of religion. It is a question that touches on one side vested interests of vast proportions, and, on another, social habits that have become rooted in custom and appetite. Add to these causes of contention, those which have arisen of late years in the realm of politics, and it is not, perhaps, to be wondered at that the subject is rarely approached in the calm spirit of philosophic inquiry. What has been written or spoken has, almost invariably, taken the form of a plea by an advocate or an assault by an adversary. There is, of course, in all public movements, an important place for impassioned appeal and invective. Light without heat is as sterile in the moral as in the physical world. But there is an equally important place for the calm and impartial consideration of facts and principles.

Prohibition is something more than a sentiment. It is a definite legislative enactment proposed as a remedy for certain ills. It is not enough to prove that those ills exist. That they do exist, proves the need of *some* remedy, and their magnitude proves the urgency of that need; but it can not prove that the remedy proposed is the proper one, nor what is the proper mode of its application.

Before Prohibition can be accepted as a remedy

for the drink-evil, three questions must be asked and answered, namely:

1. Is it in accord with wise principles of statesmanship?
2. Does it, in actual operation, give reasonable assurance of being an efficient and practicable policy?
3. Can it be attained, and at what sacrifices?

To these three questions Parts I, II, and III of this work are respectively directed.

1. The Legal Phase of the Subject.

In considering the governmental principles involved in prohibitory law, the legal and constitutional rights of government are those which naturally call for first consideration. What rights a State possesses, and what rights it is wise to exercise, are, however, entirely distinct questions. In other words, the legal right and the moral right are by no means the same. The Government has, for instance, at all times, a legal right to declare war, but not the moral right to do so, except for sufficient cause.

The legal right (without reference now to the moral right) of the government over all forms of trade and traffic is one that has been firmly established for generations. It can, under law, regulate, suppress, or destroy any form of traffic which it considers inimical to the well-being of the State. "It is the undoubted and reserved power of every "State here," said the United States Supreme

Court," as a political body, to decide * * * what "kind of property and business it will tolerate and "protect." Trade and traffic are, indeed, the outgrowth of organized society. The appetite for meat is one present to the savage; but the traffic in meat-stuffs, the barter and sale, is possible only under social organization of some sort, and social organization is possible only under some form of law. Since then, all traffic is, in a sense, the creature of law, the power of law to impose upon it whatever conditions may be necessary, has been one recognized in every form of government. It is doubtful if any State could exist that did not retain this power. As a matter of fact, a very large proportion of the acts of legislation in all governments, are but exercises of this power over the commercial transactions among its people.

It is of first importance to bear in mind that Prohibition deals with the *traffic* in liquor—with the acts of barter and sale, not the act of drinking. Practically, this distinction may amount to little; but legally it is a distinction of vital importance. The law that forbids a man to sell a certain commodity and the law that forbids him to use it, may be very wide apart in the principles of jurisprudence involved, for the act of selling is an act of public consequence, while the act of using may or may not be. The act of drinking a glass of liquor, for instance, is one that may affect no one but the man himself who drinks; but offering for sale to the public the same glass of liquor is an act that is of a public character and affects the public interest.

For four hundred years, the laws of England have recognized in the liquor traffic a proper subject for legislative action. As early as 1603 an act forbidding a publican, under the penalty of ten pounds, to allow men to stay and tipple in his house, was passed, and since then a long series of nearly five hundred regulative acts have gone on the records of English jurisprudence.

Similarly, in the United States the traffic has from the first been recognized as a fit subject for legislative action. In the Continental Congress, February 27, 1774, a resolution was passed as follows:

"*Resolved*, That it be recommended to the several legislatures of the United States immediately to pass laws the most effectual for putting an immediate stop to the pernicious practice of distilling grain, by which the most extensive evils are likely to be derived if not quickly prevented."

Here, then, in the birthplace of the American Republic, as well as in the wide variety of statute and constitutional laws, regulative, restrictive, or prohibitive, enacted in every State of the nation since, the barter and sale of liquor has been recognized as a public affair, subject to public control.

Prohibition, then, whether or not it is a wise exercise of power, would not inject any new and strange principles into our system of jurisprudence. In its legal aspect, it is an evolution, not a revolution. Every license law enacted is an assertion of the Government's right to determine the conditions on which the traffic shall exist. "I admit as inevitable," said Justice McKean, of the United States Supreme Court, "that if the State has "power to restrain by license, to any extent, she "has the discretionary power to judge of the "limit, and may go to the limit of prohibiting it "altogether."*

In the city of New York, for illustration, the Board of Excise Commissioners, in 1887, determined that the number of licenses for the sale of liquor should not be increased. (Report, Dec. 31, 1887, p. 8.) The number issued at that time was 8,817, or one for about every 160 of the population. In effect, therefore, by this determination, one hundred and fifty-nine out of one hundred and sixty persons were prohibited from selling liquors. Had any one of these one hundred and fifty-nine persons attempted to sell, he rendered himself subject to fine or imprisonment. By what principle of jurisprudence could it be maintained that the State has the legal right to prohibit one hundred and fifty-nine persons, but has not the same right to prohibit the one hundred and sixtieth person?

Indeed, the question of law is no longer open

---

* License cases, 5 Howard, 504. For similar utterances see also Cooley's Constitutional Limitations, p 727; also Bishop's Statutory Crimes, § 995.

for discussion. The Supreme Court of the United States has spoken at least twice on this question in a way that can not be mistaken. On March 6, 1847, the Court affirmed the full power of the State to regulate, restrain, or prohibit the traffic altogether. (License cases, 5 How. 504). This decision was concurred in by every member of the court, in spite of the fact that two of the most illustrious of American jurists—Daniel Webster and Rufus Choate—pleaded the case of the liquor dealers.

Another decision, equally emphatic, and on this point equally unanimous, was given by the Supreme Court December 5, 1887. (For the text of this decision, see Appendix, note A). Those who deem of importance the political character of the Court, in weighing its decisions, should not fail to note that in 1847 a majority of the justices were Democrats, and in 1887, a majority were Republicans. At two different periods, therefore, forty years apart, the highest Court of the land has unanimously affirmed the right of a State, under the Federal Constitution, to enact prohibitory law. The *legal* right in the case, then, is a settled one.

2. Two Views of the Province of Government.

But the constitutionality of a law does not prove the wisdom of it. The moral right of a Government to enact certain laws is one beyond and above the question of mere legal right. Whether Prohibition is a proper exercise of the functions of Government, is not a question to be decided by the Courts, whose duty is to interpret law as it is, rather than to decide what it should be.

From the days of Solon, the proper functions of Government have furnished to philosophers a fascinating theme for study and discussion. The old maxim, "The king can do no wrong," simplified the discussion wherever it was accepted, by making the will of the one governing the only limitation in the functions of government. But "the divine right of kings" has given way to the divine right of majorities, and the old maxim has been replaced with one that it is perhaps equally necessary to take *cum grano salis*, namely: "The voice of the people is the voice of God."

In undertaking to prescribe the limits for the government of majorities, the social philosophers of the nineteenth century have divided, broadly speaking, into two divergent schools. By one school, it is held that with the advance of civilization and the moral progress of the individual, the need for civil law grows less and less, and restraints of government should become fewer and fewer. Their view is popularly expressed in the saying: "The best government is the one "that governs least."

By the other school, it is held that the advance of civilization, the increasing density of population, and the ever-multiplying complexity of social and industrial forces, render necessary more and more legislation, defining more and more minutely the metes and bounds of individual liberty and the conditions of industrial activity.

With the advanced leaders of the former school the function of government is held to consist simply in "the administration of justice." Further than this it should not go, and cannot go without usurping rights. It should prevent or punish acts of violence and fraud—whatever is an infringement by one upon the equal rights of another. But laws fostering industry, establishing public schools, maintaining charitable institutions, guarding the public health, making public improvements and performing public services such as the carrying of mails,—all such laws are considered as beyond the proper domain of Government. Let all these affairs be left to individual effort, is the theory, and let the law attend simply to defending each man in his rights and executing justice.

The tendency of the other school is in the contrary direction. Instead of abolishing the public school system, they would add to it compulsory education. Instead of destroying the public postal service, they would re-enforce it with a postal telegraph system. Instead of calling hands off in case of industry, they would lay heavier hands on in view of the development of what they term "monopolies" and "trusts." Instead of lessening the Governmental regulation of railroads, they advocate the ultimate ownership by the Government of all lines of transportation.

Along these two divergent lines are arranged in different gradations the social philosophers of our day. At the extreme of one is the Anarchist crying for no law and no Government; at the extreme of the other is the Communist, crying for the ownership of all things by the Government.

It can be readily surmised from which direction come the objections to Prohibition. There is nothing in the *theory* of Prohibition that conflicts with the tenets of the latter school. With this school it is chiefly a question of expediency. But the adherents of the former school challenge the propriety as well as the practicability of such law. It is with them not simply a question of fact or possibility, but a question of principle.

It is the intention, in these pages, to keep the subject disentangled, as far as possible, from all questions not necessarily involved in it. Without proceeding, then, to any further comparison between the claims of these diverging schools, it is desired to look more closely into the nature of the objections brought by the former school against the principle of prohibitory law—to see, in fact, whether there is any real and necessary conflict of principles.

3. John Stuart Mill and Herbert Spencer.

The two most popular and widely read defenders of the theory that the "best government is the one that governs least," are Herbert Spencer and John Stuart Mill.

In his "Essay on Liberty," Mill defines at length what he conceives to be the proper functions of Government and the principle that should govern all legislation. He sums up his discussion of the question as follows :

"That principle is, that the sole end for which mankind are warranted, individually or collectively, in interfering with the liberty of action of any of their number, is self-protection. That the only purpose for which power can be rightfully exercised over any member of a civilized community, against his will, is to prevent harm to others. He cannot rightfully be compelled to do or forbear, because better for him to do so, because it will make him happier, because, in the opinion of others, to do so would be wise or even right. These are good reasons for remonstrating with him, or persuading him, or entreating him, but not for compelling him or visiting him with any evil in case he do otherwise. To justify that, the conduct from which it is desired to deter him must be calculated to produce evil to some one else."—(*Introduction to Essay on Liberty, p.* 23.)

The same writer again puts into still more concise form what he considers to be fundamental maxims of government. He says:

"The maxims are, first, that the individual is not accountable to society for his actions, in so far as these concern the interests of no person but himself. Advice, instruction, persuasion and avoidance by other people, if thought necessary by them for their own good, are the only measures by which society can justifiably express its dislike or disapprobation of his conduct.

"Secondly, that for such actions as are prejudicial to the interests of others, the individual is accountable, and may be subjected to either social or legal punishments, if society is of opinion that the one or the other is requisite for its protection."—(*Essay on Liberty*, p. 182.)

Almost identical with these views are those set forth by Herbert Spencer. In Social Statics, he thus defines the functions of the State:

"To enforce the fundamental law [of equal freedom]—to take care that every man has freedom to do all that he wills, provided that he infringes not the equal freedom of any other man—this is the special purpose for which the civil power exists."—(*Social Statics*, p. 341.)

Over and over he reiterates this as the central thought of his system. "The duty of the State is "—to protect—to enforce the law of equal free-"dom, to maintain men's rights, or, as we com-"monly express it—to administer justice."— (*Social Statics*, p. 280.)

Further than this, he denies that the State has any right to go, but in nothing are both Mill and Spencer more emphatic than in asserting the duty of the State to this extent. Failure here on the part of the State, failure to furnish this needed protection, is, they conceive, failure in the very end and purpose of Government. And in fact, whatever difference of opinion there may be among sociologists as to whether the sphere of Government extends *beyond* this limit, there is no difference whatever—if Anarchism be not considered—on the right and duty of Government *within* this limit.

In applying these principles, Mill, considering the rights which the State has over trade, says:

"Again, trade is a social act. Whoever undertakes to sell any description of goods to the public, does what affects the interest of other persons, and of society in general; and thus his conduct, in principle, comes within the jurisdiction of society."—(*Essay on Liberty*, p. 183.)

This extract, standing by itself, would seem to yield to the State at once the right of Prohibition. But elsewhere Mill shows that he has no intention of allowing such an application. Coming directly, in the course of his discussion, to the subject of Prohibition, he says:

"On the other hand, there are questions relating to the interference with trade which are essentially questions of liberty; such as the Maine law, already touched upon; the prohibition of the importation of opium into China; the restriction of the sale of poisons; all cases, in short, where the object of the interference is to make it impossible or difficult to obtain a particular commodity. These interferences are objectionable, not as infringements on the liberty of the producer or seller, but on that of the buyer."—(*Essay on Liberty, p.* 185.)

The idea here seems to be that since the sale of liquor, opium, and poisons, is voluntary on the part of both buyer and seller, it is not, in itself, a violation of any one's rights, and hence the State is not justified in interfering. The logic of this reasoning tells with equal force, it is evident, against *restrictive* laws as well. Mill does not hesitate to admit this. He says:

"To tax stimulants for the sole purpose of making them more difficult to be obtained, is a measure differing only in degree from their entire prohibition; and would be justified only if that were justifiable."—(*p.* 194.)

Whoever follows Mr. Mill, therefore, to the end of his logic, must, in consistency, oppose all restrictive laws and favor an unrestricted traffic in liquor. Mill explains himself farther:

" * * * * It is to this class surely [of individual acts as distinguished from social acts] that the act of drinking fermented liquors belongs. Selling fermented liquors, however, is trading, and trading is a social act. But the infringement complained of is not on the liberty of the seller, but on that of the buyer and consumer; hence the State might just as well forbid him to drink wine, as purposely make it impossible."—(*p.* 172.) Finally, in reply to a letter written by the Secretary of the United Kingdom Temperance

Alliance, in which it was argued that the drink traffic invaded his "social rights" by destroying his sense of security, by creating disorder, by increasing taxes, by hindering his free moral and intellectual development, and by weakening society, Mill says:

"A theory of social rights the like of which probably never before found its way into distinct language, being nothing short of this, that it is the absolute social right of every individual that every other individual shall act in every respect exactly as he ought; that whoever fails thereof in the smallest particular, violates my social right, and entitles me to demand from the legislature the removal of the grievance."

This, then, seems to be, in brief, the view of Mill: That Government has no right to interfere with an individual's acts, until they infringe on some other individual's rights; that the drinking of liquor does not, of itself, infringe on another's rights, and that the sale of liquor, being entirely voluntary on the part of both buyer and seller, Government has no right to interfere at the demand of some third person. In other words, if A sells liquor to B, the rights of C and D are not disturbed by the act of sale. It is true B may become drunk and then by an act of violence disturb those rights; but until he reaches that point, the law can not step in. It is the act of violence, but not the sale nor yet the drinking of the liquor, that infringed the rights of C and D. The law can forbid and punish the violence, but as there is no necessary connection between the sale of liquor and the violence, the law can not justifiably punish or forbid the sale.

So far the logic seems to be clear, and the conclusion correct, if Mill's limitations for Government be accepted. Considering each specific act of purchase and sale by itself, there seems to be in it no infringement on another's rights. But is there not something *beside* these specific acts, something antecedent to them? Before a sale is made, must there not have been, logically at least, two prior conditions established—namely, first, the facilities for trade, and, second, the permission (and protection) of organized society (Government) to conduct the proposed trade? The first of these conditions is supplied by the man himself, but the second is supplied, either tactily or explicitly, by Government. If, as Mill says, "trade is a social act," and "comes within the jurisdiction of society," is not the consent of society a logical prerequisite to the establishment of this trade? Society, indeed, does more than permit; it protects as well, by its courts and police, the trade thus established.

It becomes necessary then to go back beyond those specific acts of sale, which may not be, in themselves, and may not always involve, even in their consequences, any violation of rights, and to consider that first step necessary to be taken, namely, the consent of Government either implied or written.

If we do this, we shall find the epitomized argument now running about as follows:

A desires to sell liquor to B and others. But before doing so, since "trade is a social act" and "within the jurisdiction of society," it is necessary for him to have the consent of society and the protection it alone can give. Now, since it is agreed on all hands that the first and all-important duty of Government is " to protect—to enforce the law of equal freedom, to maintain men's rights," the first question that Government is bound to ask, before granting the protection desired, is, Will the establishment of this traffic interfere with the performance of my duty to protect the rights of my citizens?

The question then is no longer whether the specific act of selling or drinking interferes with the rights of others; but whether the traffic itself, as a whole, interferes with those rights, and with the performance of the Government's duty to protect them.

It may be objected here that if the specific acts of sale do not interfere with those rights which society is bound to protect, then the traffic as a whole does not interfere, since it is nothing but the aggregation of such sales. This, however, is a mistake. The traffic consists in much more than that, for it means not only the supplying, but the *stimulating* of a demand for liquor. It not only gratifies, but it *incites* the appetite. It not only does this in the ordinary modes of business, such as advertising and adding attractions of many sorts; but the very existence of the place of drinking is, of necessity, more or less of an incitement. If it be admitted that selling liquor to B is not violating the rights of C and D, can it be further said that *inciting B to drink* is not a violation of the rights of C and D?

Elsewhere Mill recognizes this feature of the business as an important one. He says:

"The interest, however, of these [liquor] dealers in promoting intemperance is a real evil and justifies the State in imposing restrictions and requiring guarantees which but for that justification would be infringements of legitimate liberty."

What guarantees? That they will not promote intemperance? Suppose they can not give any such guarantee (and they can not)—what then? The fact is that if the difference between restriction and Prohibition is, as Mill has said, simply a difference of degree, then in admitting that restriction is rendered justifiable by the "real "evil" of the traffic, he has admitted that Prohibition, which is but a more severe form of restriction, is rendered justifiable if the less severe form proves inadequate. But "these interferences are "objectionable," he says, "not as infringements on "the liberty of the producer or seller, but on "that of the buyer." How? By not promoting the facilities for supplying the demands of his appetite. But is the State bound to furnish facilties for supplying the demand for drink? If not, (and Mill would be the first to maintain that it is not) is the State bound to withhold legislation because it will interfere with that supply? If the duty of the State consists simply in the protection of her citizens from encroachments on their rights, it is evident that a refusal to enact laws necessary for the proper performance of that duty, solely because they will affect injuriously the gratification of appetite, is far from consistent. It is yielding, in that case, to a consideration to which, according to Mill's theory of government, it has no right even to listen.

That laws for the restriction of the liquor traffic are necessary to the proper performance of this duty of Government—a duty on which all sociologists are agreed—Mill himself admits. The same thing is implied by the legislation of all civilized Governments. It is implied by the legislation of this nation from almost the very beginning.

It must be borne in mind that in matters affecting trade, it is not, with civil government, merely a question whether to interfere or to abstain from interference. In matters of personal conduct, the question assumes that phase, but not in matters of trade. The State must either protect or prohibit here, for "trade is a social act." It must refuse permission or else grant it. Silence does not mean non-interference; it means protection in the same or similar measure as is accorded to other traffic, and the courts act on that principle when questions involving the property rights of liquor, the legality of contracts made in pursuit of the business, and similar questions arise. The trade that is not prohibited is protected.

It is quite probable, however, that the reader has discerned a difficulty in applying these reflections concerning trade to the act of manufacture. To sell, is an act of trade. To manufacture for purposes of sale, is equally an act of trade. But to manufacture an article for one's own use or enjoyment is not an act of trade. Whatever control Government can claim over the sale of liquor as a "social act," is not to be claimed over the manufacture of liquor unless it be manufacture *for sale*. On this point a valid objection can be raised by those who occupy Mill's ground, against the prohibitory laws now in force. But as a matter of fact, while the prohibitory provisions embedded in the Constitutions of Maine, Kansas and Rhode Island, do, literally construed, forbid the manufacture of liquor even for one's own use, the legislatures have never made this literal interpretation when enacting laws for the enforcement of these prohibitory clauses. The prohibition, as applied, extends only to the acts of trade.* Men may drink liquor, under Prohibition, or they may,

---

*The proposed constitutional amendment for the State of New York (Bill No. 227, in Assembly, January 26, 1888,) avoids the objection noted above. It forbids not the manufacture, but "the manufacture *for sale*."

as the law is generally construed, manufacture it for their own use. So far the claim to personal liberty is respected. It is only when they enter upon its barter and sale that the law confronts them.

4. The Question of Personal Liberty.

This distinction made by the law between the dealer and the drinker furnishes a clue to the purpose of the law. That purpose has often been conceived to be the reform of the drinker. Horatio Seymour, Governor of New York in 1854, in a message to the Legislature vetoing a bill looking toward Prohibition, stated his objection to such laws as follows:

" All experience shows that temperance, like other virtues, is not produced by law-makers, but by the influence of education, morality, and religion."

The assumption here is that the object of the law is to produce the virtue of temperance—to protect a man from his own weakness. The same idea has been stated more recently by a Congressman of the United States, as follows:

"But the attempt of one man or set of men, whether for the 'good of society' or any other cause, to reform the moral conduct of others by outward force, has always failed in the past, and always will in the future."—(*Speech in Corsicana, Texas, in* 1888, *by Roger Q. Mills, U. S. Congressman from Texas.*)

Notice the law is here described as an attempt "to reform the moral conduct by out-"ward force"—that is, to coerce a man into morality.

Samuel J. Tilden, in 1855, while a candidate for Attorney General of New York, put this same objection to prohibitory law in still more forcible language, namely :

"To-day, while it [the Democratic party] is in favor of sobriety and good morals, it disowns a system of corceive legislation which can not produce them, but must create many serious evils—which violates constitutional guarantees and sound principles of legislation—invades the rightful domain of the individual judgment and conscience, and takes a step backward toward that barbarian age when the wages of labor, the prices of commodities, a man's food and clothing, were dictated to him by a Government calling itself paternal."

These objections, it will be observed, are almost identical in nature with those urged by John Stuart Mill, and which have been considered in the preceding pages. The purpose of this prohibitory law is conceived to be "to reform moral conduct," to promote total abstinence by "coercive legisla-"tion," and believing, with Thomas Jefferson, that "the legitimate powers of Government extend to "such acts only as are injurious to others" (Thomas Jefferson, vol. viii. p. 400), Mr. Tilden and Mr. Seymour naturally object to a law which presents itself to them as an attempt to regulate a man's conduct, chiefly because it is injurious *to himself*.

It is needless to deny that their conception of the law is the one that has obtained the widest acceptance, and the objections growing out of it are the ones most frequently urged and with the strongest effect. Men everywhere resent Governmental interference with conduct which affects themselves alone. "If I want to "drink, I have the right to do it," is the popular way of putting the case. " This is a free country," said a noted orator in the heat of the last campaign, "and if a man wants to get drunk, he " has a right to do so and take the consequences." " In truth," said Lord Bramwell, of England, " these liquor laws are either to make men better " who do not want to be made better, or to make " men better who have not self-control, and in both " cases at the expense of others."

By many persons this conception of the law is accepted without hesitation. Of course it is the purpose of Prohibition, so they think, to compel men to stop drinking—what else *can* it be? It would be a genuine surprise to many to be told that any one thinks of denying that this is the purpose of the law.

Yet, as a matter of fact, the persistent iteration of this as the purpose of the law, has been met with an equally persistent denial from the leading advocates of Prohibition. It would be difficult to mention a single sustained argument for Prohibition that does not disavow any such purpose in view. Judge Pitman, of the Superior Court of Massachusetts, in his able work on "Alcohol and "the State," says: "If we have proved anything in "the course of this discussion, we have proved "exactly this: that the liquor dealer is doing "'*harm to others*'"—others, that is, than the dealer and the drinker, and this point he regards as "the *central* basis upon which the advocate of "the suppression of the liquor traffic rests his case." (*pp*. 119, 120.) He says further:

"To this extent at least [forbidding the *sale* of liquor] it seems to us that Government not only may, but *ought* to go. And no prohibitory laws yet enacted have attempted to go further." (*p*. 127.)

He makes still clearer his conception of the purpose of the law as being, not protection for the drinker from his own acts, not the reform of moral conduct, but protection to *others*, in the following words:

"The law [of Prohibition] does not propose to deal directly with the personal habits of men. It lays its hand on a traffic. Sales are public acts, and always within the domain of law. The law, for sufficient reasons of policy, prescribes the manner and modes of sales of real and personal property, makes void what it chooses, regulates what it deems dangerous, forbids, under penalties, what it thinks mischievous. If it lays either a regulating, a restraining, or a prohibiting hand upon the traffic in intoxicants, it does no differently from what it does in regard to adulterated meat, unwholesome meat, dangerous explosives, fire-works, obscene publications, lottery tickets, and numerous other subjects of sale. The only questions society asks, are: Is the trade injurious? Is it sufficiently so to call for the interference." (*pp.* 91, 92.)

John B. Finch, who was, at the time of his death, head of the Order of Good Templars and Chairman of the National Committee of the Prohibition party, advocated prohibitory law on the same principle as Judge Pitman, namely, to secure, not the reformation of the drinker, but the protection of society against the evils of drink. In his work, "The People *vs.* The Liquor Traffic," he says:

"Prohibitory liquor laws in nowise say what a man shall eat or what he shall drink. They simply aim to protect society from the pernicious influence of trade, which is a social institution. In no respect do they aim to interfere with the private liberties of the individual until those private liberties create public nuisances."

It is not necessary to add to these quotations. It is sufficient to say that the lines of reasoning on which prohibitory laws are advocated at the present time, are almost uniformly those laid down in the sentences quoted above from Judge Pitman and John B. Finch. It is true that " the reform " of moral conduct" is hoped for as a result of prohibitory legislation. It is hoped that in the absence of the usual public incitements to drink men will cease to drink; but they are not compelled to cease, not even indirectly, for the art of distillation is not so costly or difficult, but that, even under prohibitory law, households might distil their own liquor as well as bake their own bread. The farmer in Maine is accorded the undisturbed right of making cider for his family, and making it as hard as he pleases. All that Prohibition means is that the public facilities for the gratification of this appetite must cease; that the saloon shall no longer exist; and that if men insist on drinking they must satisfy their desires in some other way than through the channels of trade. This is all that the law, in itself, contemplates, and all that the advocates of the law urge. They contend that the liquor traffic has become an organized temptation; that the saloon with all its adjuncts is not in existence simply to respond to a natural craving of the appetite, but to create and to stimulate appetite; that it is impossible to strip the saloon of this inciting character except by putting an end to its very existence.

The laws against gambling, against impurity, against bribery, are advocated by many whose chief reason for advocating them is the belief that a "reform of moral conduct" will be assisted by them. It is not too far-fetched to suppose, even, that to many the chief value of laws against theft, larceny, murder, in fact laws of all kinds, lies not in the fact that they are a protection to society but that they are believed to aid in the reformation of society. Yet it would not do to stigmatize such laws as attempts " to reform the moral con-" duct of others," or to make men honest and virtuous " by a system of coercive legislation." The reform may follow, or it may even have been the object of those enacting the law; but it follows not as a coerced reformation, but as a natural result of the changed condition which the law has created. "It is the duty of Government," says Gladstone, " to make it easy to do right and hard " to do wrong." Whether or not this is accepted in its full signification, no one can claim that it is a part of the duty of Government to make it *easy to do wrong.* Yet this, in a certain sense, seems to be just what a Government does when it uses, for the barter and sale of liquor, all the powers of protection which it has at command.

In brief, while a man may claim the right to drink, on the ground that he injures nobody but himself, can he claim as his right that the saloon, which does injure somebody else, must be allowed to continue in order to supply him with drink?

5. The Sin per Se.

The right to do a thing does not, however, as has been observed, imply the wisdom of doing it. That the Government has a constitutional right, or even a philosophical and moral right to extirpate the liquor traffic, is no proof that it would be wise to exercise that right. The question of *consequences* here comes in, and ought to receive attention. The Government has the constitutional right and might have the moral right to declare war against a stronger power; yet it might be the part of wisdom, from fear of consequences, not to exercise that right. It is true that a mistaken zeal sometimes impels men into the assertion that consequences are not to be taken into consideration in determining a course of conduct. "Do "right, and trust the consequences to God," is, when rightly applied, a motto fit for a hero. But the fact is lost sight of too often, that it is only by considering the consequences that one is at times able to determine which of two courses is *right*. In many cases it is the consequences alone that determine the character of an action. Is it right or wrong to defraud your neighbor? Wrong. Why wrong? Not because of the consequences, but because of the inherent nature of the action. But is it right or wrong to drink a glass of liquor? Wrong, will again be the answer of many, but wrong *because of the consequences*, not because of the inherent sinfulness of the action. Herein lies the distinction made by the logicians and theologians between actions which are sins *per se*, that is, sins from the inherent character of the actions themselves, and those actions which are not sins *per se*, but are sins because of their consequences. To steal a dime from a rich employer may not involve much, if anything, in its consequences, but it is just as certainly sinful as though the consequences were very important. Blasphemy in the midst of a desert is as certainly a sin as blasphemy in a crowded city. The sin *per se* always results from a sinful condition of the mind or heart of the one committing it. The discussion whether it is a sin *per se* to drink a glass of liquor, grows really empty when the phrase is rightly understood. The sin of such an act must lie, if at all, in its *harmfulness*, that is, in its consequences, either on the one drinking or on others. If liquor were as *harmless* as water there would be no sin of any kind in drinking it. If it is a sin to do so, then it is because of its harmfulness. A sin *per se* indicates always a rebellion of the heart against the law of God prior to the commission of the sin. No one will claim that the drinking of wine, for instance, always indicates such an act of conscious rebellion in the mind. It *may* indicate just that; but it may *not*.

This distinction has become one of more than metaphysical importance in the present controversies. There are large religious denominations, notably the Roman Catholic Church, whose theology will not allow any tolerance, for an instant, of this Manichæan heresy that the drinking of wine is a sin *per se*. The use of the phrase becomes therefore a matter of considerable practical importance. To base the argument for Prohibition upon such a claim is almost certain to alienate a large number of the most devout church members. It is arraying religion and Prohibition in hostility instead of in alliance.

The question of Prohibition, then, is a question of consequences as well as of principles. It is not desired here, however, to enter upon the question whether Prohibition actually accomplishes the results aimed at ; that portion of the subject is reserved for Part II. What will be considered here is what consequences would follow provided Prohibition were fully secured and completely enforced.

6. The Controversy over Bible Wines.

One of the serious consequences which it is claimed would ensue, is thus stated by Rev. Dr. Howard Crosby :

"A Prohibition that would include the fermented juice of the grape would be, however we might try to explain it, a reflection upon our Lord and upon His Holy Word, which makes wine a gift of God and a token of the highest blessings. It would be a virtual declaration that we know a better way than He knew how to meet the matter of human indulgence, and that He was mistaken in His conduct and in His teaching."—(*Homiletic Review.*)

The same objection is stated by Rev. J. R. Sikes, author of "The Biblical Reason Why Prohibition is Wrong." In the preface to this work the author says :

"We lay it down as a fundamental principle that any law which makes it a criminal offense to follow the example of Jesus Christ, or live in accordance with the teachings of the Bible in matters pertaining to the personal liberty in eating and drinking, so fully guaranteed to us in the Gospel, is anti-biblical and subversive of religious as well as our civil rights. This Prohibition does * * * *"

In another place the same author says:

"In other words, which is the greater evil? The abuse of intoxicating beverages as we have it, or to destroy the faith of the masses in the Bible, as a correct rule of faith and practice, and to put in force a prohibitory law which impeaches the wisdom of God, and arraigns Jesus Christ as a criminal at a bar of human tribunal. Such are the logical and natural sequences of the Prohibition now advocated * * * *."—*p.* 36.

Naturally these objections bring us face to face with the question of Bible wines, and the dispute concerning their intoxicating qualities. As the question is, however, solely one of biblical scholarship, it is hardly desirable, nor, as will appear, necessary, to do more than briefly to indicate the nature of the controversy.

In the Old Testament two Hebrew words, *yayin* and *tirosh*, are used to designate wine. Other words are used occasionally to indicate "strong "wine," "red wine," "sweet wine," "mixed wine," and "blood of the grape," but it is about these two words that the controversy centres. An interesting fact has been observed concerning the use of these words. There are many passages where wine is spoken of as a curse and where warning is uttered against its use, such as (Proverbs xx. 1): "Wine is a mocker, strong drink is raging;" and (Proverbs xxiii. 31, 32): "Look not thou "upon the wine when it is red, when it giveth his "color in the cup, when it moveth itself aright. "At the last it biteth like a serpent and stingeth "like an adder."

In many other passages, however, wine is spoken of as a blessing, and its use is commended, such, for instance, as (Proverbs xxxi. 6): "Give "strong drink unto him that is ready to perish "and wine unto those that be of heavy hearts;" and (Isaiah lv): "Ho, every one that thirsteth "* * * come, buy wine and milk without "money and without price."

Now the word *tirosh* is never used, with one doubtful exception (Hosea iv. 11) except in those passages commendatory of wine. The word *yayin*, however, is used both in commendatory and in condemnatory passages. That there was some distinction in the minds of Old Testament writers between the word *yayin* and the word *tirosh* seems to be admitted by both sides to the discussion; but what this distinction was is the source of dispute. The advocates of the two-wine theory*, contend that *tirosh* means wine before it

---
* Among these are Prof. Moses Stuart, of Andover, Dr. Eliphalet Nott, late President of Union College, Prof. Tayler Lewis, Dr. F. R. Lees, Dr. George W. Samson.

has fermented and become intoxicating, while *yayin* is a generic term covering all kinds of wine, and meaning sometimes one kind, sometimes another, just as we use the word water to designate sometimes fresh water, sometimes salt water. Those opposing this theory regard *tirosh* as being the husbandman's name for wine, and as representing wine "in its germinant state in the "vineyard, in the process of manufacture in the "press and the vat, and, after fermentation, in its "finished state, either in the store-house, where it "was regarded as the reward of the husbandman's "care and toil, or among the tithes, where it was "expressive of gratitude to God for the fruitful-"ness of the earth."—(*Bumstead's* "*Biblical Sanction for Wine*," *p.* 67.) The word *yayin*, it is held, was "the common every-day word for wine; "the word of the consumer, the entertainer, the "merchant, as *tirosh* was the word of the husband-"man and manufacturer."—(*Ibid. p.* 71.) These opponents of the two-wine theory claim, of course, that *tirosh* and *yayin* were both fermented, and that there is no sanction whatever for the view that *tirosh* was an unfermented wine.

In the New Testament, the Greek word almost invariably used to designate wine is *óinos*. There is the same dispute concerning this that exists concerning *yayin*, one side contending that it was a generic term, meaning sometimes fermented and sometimes unfermented wine, the other side contending that it means, wherever used, fermented wine.

From this brief statement of the controversy, it will be seen that to ask for a decision on this question either from a legislature or by popular vote, would be about as appropriate as to ask for a decision from the same source on the question, Who built the pyramids? or Where was Homer born? It is clearly a question to be settled by biblical and philological students among themselves. All that can be asked, in the matter of legislation, is that it be such as *will not force either side to violate their convictions of religious duty*. To ask that a Legislature shall refuse to prohibit the sale of liquor on the ground that Jesus drank it, is as manifestly improper as to ask that it prohibit the sale on the ground that Jesus did not drink it. Surely the Legislature, or the people, are not called upon to settle a controversy of this sort when considering whether public interest demands the extinction of the liquor traffic of to-day.

If Prohibition conflicts with the religious duties —or what are conceived to be such—of either side to the controversy, this is, of course, a serious objection. But no one claims that the use of wine, except at the Sacrament of the Lord's Supper, is ever a religious *duty*. As a matter of fact, all prohibitory laws yet adopted or submitted for adoption (with one exception, in Michigan, and that the result of an oversight) have excepted from their provisions the use of liquor for sacramental purposes, and the sale for such use. Prohibition, therefore, conflicts with no religious duties. The most that can be said is that it deprives many of a *privilege* which the teaching of Scripture and the example of Christ (as they conceive) gives them the right to enjoy or not as they wish. In other words, because they believe that Christ drank fermented wine nineteen centuries ago, they demand not only that the State give them the right to drink (which it does, even under Prohibition), but shall continue to authorize the prosecution of the traffic, at whatever jeopardy to public interests, in order that they may supply themselves with drink.

If Prohibition is a reflection upon Christ, as Dr. Crosby maintains, is not total abstinence equally a reflection upon Christ? Is it not even much more of a reflection upon him? The law declares that, for the safety of public interests, the *traffic* in liquor must cease (Christ never engaged in the traffic), while total abstinence, which is enjoined as a duty by certain of the largest religious denominations, forbids, for similar reasons of expediency, the *drinking* of liquor except for medicinal purposes. If, indeed, the doctrine of total abstinence or the law of Prohibition implied that the drinking or the making of liquor is, like stealing, a sin *per se*, an act inherently wrong, then there would be an implication that Christ, if he made and drank fermented wine, had committed a sin. But there is, of a certainty, no such implication either in the doctrine or the law, no matter what opponents or injudicious friends of either may say. Such a conception of law would bring us at once into antagonism to an almost countless array of civil ordinances and statutes which forbid acts not sinful in themselves but dangerous to the welfare of society.

"An act may be declared criminal," says Pike's History of Crime (vol. II, p. 492) "which is "not, even in the same age, regarded as in "itself immoral, and another may be considered "immoral which does not involve any legal pen- "alties."

Dr. Herrick Johnson has, undoubtedly, the best of legal authority for the reply he has made to Dr. Crosby in the following words:

"The legal prohibition of an act is solely on the ground of *its evil effects upon society*, and not at all on the ground of *the inherent evil of the act itself*. Public law does indeed make a distinction between the things it prohibits, classifying them as evils in themselves (*mala in se*) and evils prohibited (*mala prohibita*); but the ground of their prohibition is exactly the same. Homicide, an act evil in itself (*malum in se*), is prohibited. So the building a frame house within the fire limits of a city, an act not evil in itself, is prohibited. There is inherent moral wrong in homicide. There is no inherent moral wrong in building a frame house. But the law seeks to prevent the one as well as the other, *solely to protect society.* * * Clearly the inherent rightfulness or wrongfulness of an act has nothing whatever to do with prohibition of it by law. *The amount and character of the evil effects upon others* are what determine whether any given thing shall be prohibited or not. If the evils are open, public, imperiling public interests, disturbing public order, endangering property or human life, then the ground is furnished for prohibition. Ten thousand things are wrong in themselves that the law never touches, and never ought to touch; while things right and innocent in themselves, the law often prohibits."

" The evil effects upon others " is the ground here laid down by Dr. Johnson for Prohibition of the liquor traffic. " General reasons of public " utility " is the phrase Judge Cooley uses when speaking, in his great work on " Constitutional " Limitations " (p. 728) of the basis on which laws restricting or prohibiting the traffic in liquor rest. Chief Justice Shaw, of Massachusetts, (case of Fisher *vs.* McGirr) refers to the same class of laws as enacted because the acts which they forbid " would be injurious, dangerous, or obnoxious," not because they would be sinful or even immoral. And, finally, the Supreme Court of the United States speaks of prohibitory laws, not as a declaration, in any wise, regarding the moral character of the drinking or selling of liquor, but as an " effort to guard the community against the evils attend-

"ing the excessive use of such liquors," (*Mugler vs The State of Kansas* and *The State of Kansas vs Ziebold and Hagelin.*)

That there is anything in the principal of prohibitory law which conflicts with the doctrines of Scripture, as Rev. Mr. Sikes asserts, regarding personal liberty in eating and drinking, seems equally untenable. The law of the Jews forbade the use of pork, and neither the Old Testament Scriptures, nor the words of Christ ever indicated that that law was offensive to divine truth. There seem to many to be reasons equally as good for the Prohibition of the liquor *traffic* in our day as there were for Prohibition of the *use* of pork in the days of Christ.

It is difficult to see, therefore, how the controversy over Bible wines in use in the days of the prophets, or those in use in the days of Christ can properly affect the question whether the State, in the exercise of its police power, should put an end to the traffic in liquors as a menace to the welfare and safety of society. By so doing it prevents no conduct which Christ ever enjoined upon his followers as a duty. His diet was never ordained as a diet for his disciples. If food which he ate or liquid which he drank is found by the Christian of to-day injurious or distasteful, he rejects it himself, or prohibits it for his family, with no thought of casting any "reflection" on the Saviour. If any article of Christ's diet is found to be to-day, through the weakness of men, or the peculiarity of the climate, or any other reason, a source of wide-spread mischief, can not the State with equal propriety forbid the public traffic therein?

7. The Physiological Effects of Alcohol.

But it is not into the realms of philosophy and religion alone that this question leads us. The scientific controversy has been still more exhaustive and exhausting. If the importance of a subject, like the importance of a city, is indicated by the number of avenues of approach to it, this subject must be one of the greatest.

Perhaps the most elaborate argument ever made against Prohibition was that delivered in 1867 before the Joint Special Committee of the Massachusetts Legislature, by ex-Governor John A. Andrew. Mr. Andrew was employed as counsel for those petitioning the Legislature for a repeal of the prohibitory law then on the statute books of that State. Almost his entire address consisted in an assault upon two positions which he assumed to be the basis of Prohibition, namely, the " essentially poisonous character of alcoholic bev-" erages," and " the immorality of their use." To disprove these two propositions Mr. Andrew expended all his force, showing the shrewdness of the attorney rather than the wisdom of the philosopher. For the supposition that Prohibition rests upon either or both these propositions is one that, to say the least of it, needs to be shown rather than assumed.

Nevertheless, the question regarding the physiological effects of alcoholic liquors is one that lies very near to the subject in hand and demands attention. If alcoholic liquors are of considerable dietetic value—valuable, that is to say, not simply for occasional use as a medicine, but as a part of one's regular diet—then any law interfering with such use involves consequences that can not be overlooked. The grounds of controversy can be briefly stated, and those points on which there is practical agreement and those on which there is difference of opinion readily seen.

In 1842, the renowned chemist, Baron Liebig, propounded a theory with regard to food, which has since, with some recent modifications, retained the general acceptance of physiologists of the world. His theory, briefly stated, comprised the division of all foods into two classes, namely, *plastic foods*, or those which aid in building up the structures of the body; and *respiratory foods*, or those which aid in producing heat. In all the plastic, or structure-building, foods, it was found that nitrogen was contained as an important element. The respiratory foods were found to be hydro-carbons, which undergo oxidation in the system, and thus aid in furnishing heat and force.

In making his classifications, Liebig classified alcohol as a respiratory food ("Animal Chemistry," p. 35) expressly stating that it was not a structure-building food since it had "no element capable of "entering into the composition of blood, muscular fibre, or any part which is the seat of the vital principle." It was considered a heat-producing food however, since it contains both hydrogen and carbon, and inasmuch as its use is followed by an increase of heat on the surface of the body.

This classification of alcohol was accepted with but little or no dissent, until thirty years later, when two French scientists, Lallemand and Perrin, assisted by Duroy, published the results of a series of experiments which they had conducted. In these experiments, they claimed to have discovered two facts, namely, (1) that alcohol, unchanged by combustion or in any other way, was eliminated from the system in the breath, in the excretions, and by the skin; and (2) that none of the derivatives, such as aldehyde and acetic acid, which are formed in the combustion of alcohol, were to be found anywhere in the system. Their conclusion, therefore, was that alcohol did not undergo combustion, but was expelled *in toto*, as an intruder, from the body.

This conclusion was, in turn, generally accepted, until several years later still, when Dr. Anstie, of England, and, after him, Drs. Thudichum, Schulinus, and Dupre, announced the result of a series of experiments, covering a number of years. They made careful comparison between the amount of alcohol administered to living animals, and the amount which was to be found afterward in the various excretions of the body. In one case the animal was put to death suddenly two hours after the alcohol was administered, and an analysis was made of every part of the body—bone, fiber, hair, and all. (See The Practitioner for July, 1874.)

The result was that while a portion of the alcohol was in each case found to be unchanged by combustion, this was but a fraction of the entire quantity administered. The rest, it was concluded, underwent change, in some way, within the system, and the inference generally drawn was that, as Liebig had announced, it was changed by combustion, and thus aided in the production of heat. Alcohol was at once restored, then, to the rank of a respiratory food.

Still another series of experiments threw additional light on the subject. As early as 1850, Dr. N. S. Davis, of Chicago, (afterward President of the American Medical Association, and, in 1887, President of the International Medical Association which convened in Washington) had conducted a series of careful experiments which appeared to indicate " that the presence of alcohol actually reduced the temperature of the body." * Thirteen years later (1863) Dr. B. W. Richardson, F. R. S., undertook, at the request of the British Association for the Advancement of Science, a series of very elaborate experiments on the effects of nitrate of amyl, which led him into a special study of the properties of alcohol. The result was as stated in his " Ten Cantor Lectures "

---

* " Alcoholic Liquors in the Practice of Medicine." p. 3.

(p. 116) that he found the administration of alcohol to a living animal to be followed by an actual *reduction*, instead of increase, of the products of combustion; and that in every stage of effect, the general temperature of the animal was *lowered* instead of raised. His conclusion was that alcohol does not undergo combustion, since no trace can be found of either the products or the effects of it. In other words, as laconically expressed by Dr. F. R. Lees: " no ashes; no fire."

But the point of controversy shifted. It has been known for many years that one of the effects of alcohol is to reduce the amount of waste tissue which is eliminated from the system. All the processes of animal life are attended with the destruction, as is well known, of cellular tissue, and its elimination from the system. It is agreed that alcohol reduces the amount eliminated, but the way in which it effects this has become now the central point of controversy. The view held by Dr. Wm. B. Carpenter, Dr. N. S. Davis, Dr. Richardson and others is that this effect is accomplished by "obstructing the removal of the effete "matter of the tissues" (Address of Dr. Carpenter in Tremont Temple, Boston, Dec. 3, 1882.) The view held, on the contrary, by Prof. J. F. W. Johnson, Dr. Hammond, and others is that alcohol really retards the destruction of the tissue, and in this way effects a saving of material. It is conceded, however, that no such retardation of the natural processes of life is desirable in time of health; but in time of disease, and especially in certain fevers, it is claimed that alcohol, by retarding the oxygenation and the undue wasting of the tissue, acts as a valuable remedial agent.

Such is a mere outline, touching only the more salient points, of a controversy which has waged more or less intermittently for a generation, and given birth to numerous volumes; but which has not by any means been settled. It may be said, perhaps, that there is practical agreement on the statement made by Dr. Willard Parker, in his Preface to Dr. Richardson's "Ten Cantor Lec-"tures," namely, that "alcohol has no place in the "healthy system;" but the value of this agreement is modified by the fact that few people are in a state of perfect health. One other point of practical agreement is this, that alcohol is at times useful for medicinal purposes, but at just what times and in just what quantities is something on which there is a wide variance of professional opinion. Some advise it as a daily tonic for many different kinds of ailments, while others claim that it can be dispensed with altogether, the editor of the Boston Journal of Chemistry, Dr. J. R. Nichols, going so far as to claim that there is no use to which alcohol is put for which a less hazardous and equally efficacious substitute has not been found.

When the doctors differ, who shall decide? Evidently each doctor must decide for himself, in cases of his own. This difference of professional opinion is not peculiar to alcohol; it extends, to a greater or less extent, to nearly every drug in the *Materia Medica*. Legislatures can not decide this scientific question any better than the bibical question. They can do nothing else than recognize the disagreement, and leave each doctor free to administer this drug, alcohol, as he is free to administer other dangerous drugs, such, for instance, as morphine and laudanum. If legislation does this, it certainly does all that science can possibly ask.

Does prohibitory legislation give this freedom to physicians?

There can be no doubt that it is the design of the law so to do, though that design has at times been imperfectly carried out. Every prohibitory law yet passed, or submitted to the people, has made an exception of liquors sold for medicinal purposes, and allowed such sale under what were deemed necessary regulations. These regulations vary in different States. In Maine a town agent is appointed by the Selectmen of any town, or by the Mayor and Board of Aldermen of any city, who receives a compensation fixed by the board appointing him, and whose duty it is to sell the liquor demanded for medicinal, mechanical, and manufacturing purposes. But "no such agent shall "have any interest in such liquors or in the profits "of the sale thereof."–(*Chapter* 140, *Laws of Maine*, 1887.) In Massachusetts, town and city agents were similarly appointed under the prohibitory law on the statute-books from 1855 to 1867; but with this difference, that in Maine the liquor is purchased by the appointing board, from a State commissioner, whose salary is fixed, and the agent is supplied by the board; while in Massachusetts the State commissioner, appointed by the Governor, supplied the town agents direct throughout the State. A State assayer was also appointed who analyzed the liquor purchased by the Commissioner and certified to its purity. Both Commissioner and Assayer were paid, not by fixed salaries, but by certain commissions on all sales. The result was frequent complaint both of the quality of liquor and the price, and the dissatisfaction with these provisions led the faculty of the College of Pharmacy in Boston to petition in 1867 for a repeal of the law.

In Iowa and Kansas registered pharmacists alone are allowed to sell liquor, and they can sell only to applicants who present an application signed by a physician and by the applicant, setting forth the kind and amount of liquor desired, and the purpose for which it is required. A record of sales must be kept by the pharmacist and submitted at intervals to the probate judge. Under the law requiring pharmacists to pass an examination before being registered, an efficient safeguard is maintained against the conversion of saloons into pseudo-drugstores, and the continuance, under such a disguise, of the outlawed business.

What the law, then, designs to accomplish, and, more or less successfully, does accomplish, is not to deprive physicians of the right to administer alcohol as they see fit, but to place the administering of it *wholly in their hands*, and to let their judgment determine in each case, not the judgment of the drinker himself. If alcohol is, indeed, of special medicinal or dietetic value, certainly science has nothing to gain from each individual's determining for himself just how much alcohol he ought to have, how often he ought to take it, and in what form, whether as beer, brandy, gin, whiskey, or some other form. Certainly the doctors would be the first to deplore any such loose method in the use of any other powerful drug; but in the case of alcohol such use is rendered doubly unscientific by its attractions for the appetite and its delusions for the mind. Prohibitory law, therefore, does, to the extent to which it succeeds in carrying out its design, reinforce medical science and *vindicate*, instead of challenging, its rights.

In the preceding pages, it will have been observed, no attempt has been made to state anything but the negative side of the question. Attention has been given not so much to the considerations urged in behalf of Prohibition, as to the objections urged against it. If the views so far set forth are correct ones, then the *a priori* objections to Prohibition on legal, philosophical, scriptural and scientific grounds, are in reality baseless, and founded in misconception.

The question still remains, why should this one form of traffic be singled out, and, except within very narrow limits, forbidden by law?

Every form of traffic is attended with more or less of evil effects. The traffic in dry-goods and that in jewelry may incite to extravagance. The traffic in staples may lead to speculative excesses. That in railroad stocks may give birth to stock-jobbing iniquities. Yet no one proposes the prohibition of these forms of traffic, nor even proposes such restrictions as are likely to cripple them seriously. Why then is such a severe restriction proposed for the traffic in alcoholic liquors? An adequate answer can be found only by showing:

That the evil effects of the drink traffic, as compared to its benefits, are of exceptional magnitude and gravity.

That these evil effects are practically inseparable from the traffic.

That these evil effects are by no means confined to those who participate in the traffic, either as buyers or sellers of drink, but extend, in a serious degree, to society in general.

We come then to a consideration of the effects of the drink traffic, their nature and their extent. For purposes of convenience, these effects may be divided into three classes, as follows:

1. The moral and physical effects, including the relation of drink to vice, crime, and disease.

2. The economic effects, including the relation

of drink to industrial conditions, to taxation, and to pauperism.

3. The political effects of drink and the associations inseparable from it.

8. Drink and Crime.

In considering the evidence concerning the connection between drink and crime, one is embarrassed chiefly by the multitude of testimonies from judges, police officers, keepers of prisons, jails, and reformatory institutions, and the agents of charitable institutions. As a rule, these testimonies have been gratuitously given, called forth either by some unusual experience or by the inquiries of temperance societies. Under such circumstances the objection might be raised that, in the main, these testimonies represent *extraordinary* rather than ordinary experiences. Men with a startling experience on this subject are more likely to call public attention to it than those whose experience has been commonplace. This must be borne in mind frequently in weighing such testimonies, and in reaching general conclusions. But no such discount need be made in the case of official investigations, when men appear, not of their own volition, but in response to official summons. Unfortunately, such investigations have been almost unknown in this country. For many years the attempt has been made to secure from Congress a Commission of Inquiry, but the attempts have been steadily thwarted in the lower House. It is impossible for private enterprise to supply the place of such a commission, since there would be no power to summon witnesses and command their compliance.

In England, however, different treatment has been accorded the subject. Probably the fullest investigation ever made into the results of intemperance was instituted in 1876, by a Special Committee appointed by the House of Lords. The evidence laid before that committee is published in four large quarto volumes, and covers not only the United Kingdom, but many of the countries in Continental Europe. Most of the testimony taken in detail related to the four large cities of London, Liverpool, Manchester and Birmingham. Valuable figures were, however, obtained for all of England, Scotland, and Wales.

It appears that in the Metropolitan Police District (London and outlying districts) in the year ending in 1876, the number of arrests for "drunk and incapable" and for "drunk and disorderly" was 32,328 (Second Rep., App. K., p. 393,) nearly one-half of these (15,558) being females. All the cases of assault and disorder, numbering 16,713 (Third Rep., App. D., p. 314,) were, with the exception of 227, committed by persons under the influence of drink. Judge Davis, counsel for the Police Commissioners of London, in the course of a long and valuable statement, said:

"Speaking of the absolute amount of drunkenness, of course I do not dispute for a moment (it would be merely repeating what judges say over and over again) the great connection there is, beyond doubt, between the charges of drunkenness and all those associated street offenses and real crimes, from simple assaults to assaults with instruments, stabbing, wounding, and so forth, resulting in death, involving charges of manslaughter, or murder, as the case may be; that is obviously so."—(*First Rep.*, *p.* 123.)

In the city of Liverpool, the statistics presented to the Commission by Wm. Hoyle, a statistical specialist, show that out of 62,831 persons arrested in Liverpool in the two years 1871-'73, for crimes of all kinds, two-thirds (41,042) were drunk when arrested, the proportion being about three men to two women.—(*Third Rep.*, *App. B.*, *p.* 311.) It is not, perhaps, just to claim that every crime committed while under the influence of drink is due to drink as a sole cause; but with few, if any, exceptions, it must be regarded as an auxiliary cause. The number of arrests due solely to the cause of drink was only about one-half the above number.

In Manchester, during the five years 1868-1872, inclusive, the total number of those arrested for all causes and brought before the magistrates, was 106,424. Of this number nearly one-third (32,785) were charged with drunkenness, but more than twice that number, or nearly two-thirds (67,802) were drunk when arrested.—(*Third Rep. App. B.*, *p.* 311.) The following is a brief extract from the testimony of the Head Constable of Manchester; (First Rep., p. 171.)

Q. 1664. Do you connect many of the crimes of violence which come under the notice of the police with drunkenness?

I connect crimes of violence with drunkenness, undoubtedly.

Q. 1665. Does that apply to no other forms of crime?

Drunkenness leads to loss of work and very often to theft, but assault and crimes of violence are mostly in connection with drunkenness.

In the testimony regarding Birmingham, an important fact was developed in the testimony of ex-Mayor Sir Joseph Chamberlain, now the leader of the Liberal Unionists. He stated that on a Saturday evening a short time previous, special watchers, for whose character he vouched, had kept tally of the persons coming out of thirty-five fairly representative public houses in different parts of the city, between the hours of eight and twelve. Their reports showed 15,057 persons (9,351 males, 5,706 females) coming out in the specified time, of whom 838 were visibly drunk. Yet the police returns showed that there were in the entire city, during the twenty-four hours of the same day, but twenty-nine arrests for drunkenness. "If to-morrow it were necessary for any "purpose," said Mr. Chamberlain, "I could under-"take to have the statistics of Birmingham made "ten times as bad as they were before; just one "turn of the screw would bring in ten times the "number [of arrests for drunkenness]."—(*Second*

Rep. p., 235.) This indicates pretty clearly that whatever inaccuracies there may be in police reports on this point, in England, at least, they certainly do not *overstate* the truth about drunkenness.

It was, in fact, indicated by the testimony of the police officials that the uniform practice is not to arrest every man who is drunk, but only those who are creating a disturbance or who are incapable of walking safely along the street. So that there is no risk whatever taken in assuming that each case of drunkenness that appears on these records stands for a public disturber or a public nuisance.

The total number of arrests for drunkenness in England and Wales, in 1875, according to figures obtained by the Committee of the House of Lords, was 203,989 (*Final Rep. p. xxxiv*), having increased to that number from 88,361 in 1860. This means a proportion of one public offense, due solely to drink, to each 112 of population. In addition to these were offenses committed under the influence of drink, and in which it must be reckoned as an auxiliary cause, and which, in the cities of Liverpool and Manchester (the only cities from which figures were furnished for a comparison on this point), equalled the number of arrests for which drink was the sole cause.

The statistics furnished the committee for Scotland give, in twenty-six counties, the number of total arrests for all crimes, and the number of those who were drunk when arrested. In these counties, with a combined population of 1,565,803, the total of arrests for three years, 1874–'75–'76, was 66,346. More than one-half (34,806) were drunk when arrested. These counties, too, were chiefly rural districts, fifteen having a population of less than 50,000 and but four having a population of over 100,000. In these rural counties, therefore, there was, on an average, one public offense (not counting of course those undetected by the police) each year, due to drink as either the sole or an auxiliary cause, for every 135 of population. How large the number of such offenses is which, either in the cities or rural districts, are unnoticed by the police, can only be surmised.

Statistics of this sort for the United States can be obtained in piecemeal only, and at considerable difficulty. One of the minor disadvantages of our republican form of government is that criminal statistics are kept on a sort of "go-as-you-please" plan, so that in certain cities while the figures will be kept with care from year to year, in others the police officials can give the figures for their term of office only. The Prison Reform Association, it is understood, is striving for some improvement in this matter, but as yet the best that can be done apparently is to consider the figures for a number of fairly representative cities scattered throughout the country.

In "The Political Prohibitionist for 1887," compiled by W. W. Spooner and C. De F. Hoxie, a table is published (p. 59) giving the number of arrests in 1886 for all causes, the number of arrests for drunkenness, and the number of arrests for drunkenness, disorderly conduct, and assault combined, for 58 cities of the Union. The figures were obtained partly from the published reports of police officials and partly from direct correspondence with them. In these 58 cities (see Appendix, note B.), in 17 different States, with a total population (6,316,572) of more than one-tenth the entire population of the country, the total number of arrests for all causes was 304,478, and of these 191,460 were for drunkenness, drunkenness and disorderly conduct, and assaults. From this a very small reduction should be made for assaults not due to drink. *From these figures it appears that in these fifty-eight cities, for every thirty-four of the population, there was one offense against public order and decency, due solely to drink, comprising more than three-fifths of all the offenses for which the police were called on to intervene.*

It seems to be unnecessary, with official evidence of this kind in hand, to recall the testimonies made public in such abundance by judges, police officers, grand juries, and wardens and chaplains of penal institutions. This testimony varies, in the precise proportions of crime estimated as due to drink, but it is unanimous on the general fact that a *large* proportion of the crimes of violence are due directly to drink, and that many other crimes are due to it as an auxiliary cause.

One thing especially should be noted: That these public offenses due to drink are of precisely that class which it is the first duty of Government to guard against, namely, offenses against personal safety and public order. So overmastering does even Herbert Spencer consider the duty of Government to furnish protection in these respects, that he contends for a citizen's right, if the State fails in its duty at this point, to release himself from all obligations to aid in its support. The crimes of violence are the very ones which figure most largely in the count against drink, next to the crime of simple drunkenness which is, in itself, a public nuisance and disturbance.

In its efforts to guard against these crimes, the State deals now chiefly with the drunkard, not with the traffic. Whatever truth there may be in the saying, "You can't make a man sober by act "of Parliament," applies to the present policy of the State, rather than to the policy of Prohibition, which is an effort to guard against these evils by dealing with a *traffic*, not an appetite. It is somewhat surprising to find how often this objection has been advanced for the perpetuation of the present policy of the State, with which it is, rightly considered, in direct opposition, and for the defeat of the very policy which is most in harmony with it.

9. Drink and Death.

The relation between drink and mortality, it has seemed impossible to ascertain with anything like scientific accuracy. This is not from the lack of proper effort, but is due to the nature itself of this relation. Intemperance, in and of itself, is very rarely the immediate cause of death. In drinking alcoholic liquors, stupefaction almost always overtakes the drinker before he has swallowed enough liquor to kill. Except in the comparatively few cases of outright alcoholism, intemperance in drink is a mediate rather than an immediate cause of death. While the number of deaths due to immediate causes, such as consumption, pneumonia, typhoid fever and the like, may be determined with approximate accuracy from vital statistics, it is hardly more possible to tell, with any close approach to accuracy, from ordinary sources of information, how many cases of death are due to intemperance in drink, than to tell how many are due to intemperance in eating. We know that bad sanitation and bad ventilation are causes in many instances of death, but they are not immediate causes, and in consequence do not figure on the death-records. It would be obviously absurd for one looking through the census reports and finding that none of the deaths enumerated are attributed to bad sanitary conditions, to conclude that these are in nowise a cause of mortality. It would be equally absurd to adopt such a course of reasoning in reference to intemperance.

Many efforts have been made to ascertain the ratio of mortality due to drink by comparisons between the death-rate of total abstainers and that of drinkers. In a paper read by E. Vivian, M. A., before the British Association for the Advancement of Science, in 1875, there was given the result of statistics kept by the United Kingdom and General Provident Institution—a life insurance society. By keeping total abstainers in a class by themselves, it was found that the deathrate among them was considerably less than that among the moderate drinkers. Similar comparison has been made, with a similar result, between the Ancient Order of United Workingmen, in Manchester, England, and the Order of Good Templars, as also between the Odd Fellows' Association and the Good Templars. But all these and similar comparisons, while they furnish ground for a reasonable presumption against drink, are of little worth in furnishing scientific data.

Even if we knew the exact ratio of mortality among all the total abstainers of the nation, and that among all the drinkers, it would be altogether unwarranted to assume that the difference was due solely to drink. Intemperance is almost invariably associated with other vices or conditions that operate as auxiliary causes of disease and death, while the same habit of self-restraint which the total abstainer has cultivated is likely to operate in respect to other indulgences and to prolong his life for reasons aside entirely from the effects of drink.

An investigation has been made, within the last few years, by the British Medical Association, which, all things considered, is the most scientific and valuable ever made public in regard to this question. Its value is increased by the fact that it was made by a purely scientific body in the interests of no theory or trade.

The inquiry was conducted by a special committee of the association, from May 9, 1885, to December 11, 1886. Each of the contributors to the inquiry, being in each case a member of the association, was requested to take his death-certificate book for the preceding three years, and from the counter-foils of the certificates of males over twenty-five years of age, to fill in the blank inquiries sent out by the committee. These inquiries covered the following particulars among others: Occupation during life, habits in regard to alcoholic drinks, age at death, and the immediate cause or causes of death. Responses were received from 178 members of the association, giving the desired data for 4,234 cases of death. The responses were tabulated by the committee, and a full report of the inquiry published in the British Medical Journal, June 23, 1888.

The result is a curious one, and forcibly illustrates what has been said about the fallacy underlying a mere comparison between the mortality rate among abstainers and that among drinkers, but in this case the fallacy tells against the abstainers.

In the returns, the 4234 cases of death were divided, according to habits in respect of drink, into five classes, namely:

(1) Total abstainers; (2) The habitually temperate drinkers; (3) The careless drinkers, those who usually drink in moderation, but occasionally indulge to excess; (4) The free drinkers, men who are not inebriates, and yet drink constantly "more than is good for them;" (5) The decidedly intemperate inebriates. Table ix shows the average age at death of each class, from which it appears that the average age among total abstainers was even lower than that among the decidedly intemperate. The figures given are as follows:

Total abstainers—average age at death—51.22 yrs.
Habitually temperate "   " "   "   —62.13 "
Careless drinkers   "   " "   "   —59.67 "
Free drinkers   "   " "   "   —57.59 "
Decidedly intemperate " " "   "   —52.03 "

This would seem to indicate that the longevity of total abstainers is nearly eleven years less than that of the moderate drinkers, and less than that of any other class, less even than that of the drunkards. This is explained by the Committee, in part, by the fact that "the class of total "abstainers is somewhat differently constituted "from any of the other classes," inasmuch as the "total abstinence movements which have played so "important a part in this country [England] of "late years have made many more converts "among the young than among the middle-aged "or elderly." But there is another fact which serves to invalidate not only the comparison as it pertains to the total abstainers, but, in less degree, as it pertains to all the other classes as well.

Let a community be conceived in which all males between the ages of 15 and 25 are total abstainers; all who learn to drink habitually, and in moderation, begin to do so not earlier than the age of 25; all who learn to drink freely begin to do so not sooner than the age of 35; and all who become habitually intemperate become so not sooner than the age of 45. Now let a comparison be instituted between these different classes, in order to ascertain the average age at death in each class. It is of course apparent that there could not be a single death at an earlier age than 45 chronicled among the intemperate, because there were no intemperate persons less than 45 years of age. There would be no deaths at an earlier age than 35 among the free drinkers, none earlier than 25 among the temperate drinkers, while every death earlier than 25 would be the death of a total abstainer. It is needless to point out that such a comparison would show a higher average age among the intemperate than among any other class.

Now a condition of things somewhat similar to this supposed condition does actually exist. As the report of the Committee points out, the alcoholic habit tends to increase from youth up to about 45 or 50 years of age. It follows that the average age of the class of total abstainers living at any period would be much lower than that of the drunkards. Both by reason of the fact stated in the report about the number of young men who are converts to the doctrine of total abstinence, and by reason of the presence of home influences and the absence of that strain and stress that drive many to the cup in later years, the comparison is rendered worthless so far as the class of total abstainers is concerned, and is so confessed in the report. "We have not in these returns," says the Committee, "the means of coming to any "conclusion as to the relative duration of life of "total abstainers and habitually temperate "drinkers of alcoholic liquors."

The same considerations affect, in a less degree, the comparisons between other classes. Whatever inaccuracies there are, however, because of this, tell in favor of the harder drinkers. The difference given (over ten years) between the average age at death of the habitually temperate and the habitually intemperate, tells therefore *less* than the truth. But on the basis of these figures we may assert broadly, that the report shows that those who become intemperate after the age of twenty-five, lose, on an average, ten years out of the thirty-five that they otherwise have to live, and that the free drinkers lose five years out of the thirty-five.

But the report is of greater value in a direction that seems not to have suggested itself at all to the Committee. We have in it a means of determining at last, with some respectable degree of accuracy, the number of deaths due to drink, and, with less accuracy, the number of intemperate drinkers.

In the 4234 deaths reported, all classes and conditions of society were represented, and all sections of the country as well. Now the total number of deaths in England and Wales, in 1886, of males over 25 years of age, was 261,066, out of a population of 27,870,586. The deaths, then, of 4234 males over 25 years of age in three years' time, would represent a population of 150,000, which, so far as drink is concerned, may be considered a representative population. Out of these 4234 deaths, 1645 were temperate drinkers, 1122 were careless drinkers, 653 were free drinkers, and 653 were habitually intemperate. If the same ratio held good for the entire nation, as for this population of 150,000, we should have the following as the number of deaths each year among these four different classes:

Temperate drinkers, males over 25, dying (from all causes) each year	101,430
Careless drinkers, males over 25, dying (from all causes) each year	69,111
Free drinkers, males over 25, dying (from all causes) each year	40,263
Habitually intemperate drinkers, males over 25, dying (from all causes) each year	40,263

To compute the number of living persons in each class is a more difficult matter, but having the number of deaths in each class and the *comparative* mortality, we can, by algebraic formulæ (see Appendix, Note C) compute this also. The result will be, for the last two classes of drinkers, as follows:

Males over 25, in England, belonging to class of "free drinkers"	903,917
Males over 25, in England, belonging to class of "habitually intemperate"	759,922
Total hard drinkers	1,663,839

That is to say, out of a total population in England and Wales, in 1886, of 27,870,586, there were 1,663,839 males over 25 years of age who were accustomed to excessive drinking, to the point of frequent drunkenness; and among these there were, from all causes, 80,526 deaths.

In these figures females are not included. The police statistics indicate that in England one-half as much drunkenness is found among females as among males*. This would give:

Number of hard drinkers in England (male)	1,633,839
Number of " " " (female)	831,919
Total	2,465,758

The number of deaths among these, due to all causes, was (reckoning the same ratio among females as among males†) about 120,000.

So far we can go with some feeling of approxi-

---

* In Liverpool the proportion of arrests for drunkenness is 4 females to 6 males; in London, 7 to 8; in Manchester, less than 4 to 9.

† This ratio should in all probability be higher, as drink is more destructive to woman. If one attempts to fix on any other ratio however, it must be largely a matter of guess-work.

mate certainty. The reasons rendering the Committee's report unreliable in other respects do not affect the calculations regarding the total number of deaths of intemperate persons. But when we endeavor to ascertain the proportion of these deaths due to drink itself, we become involved in the inaccuracies already pointed out. If the comparisons made in the report, between the mortality of temperate and the mortality of intemperate drinkers were strictly accurate (and whatever error there is tells in favor of the intemperate) the ratio of mortality among the hard drinkers is one-fourth greater than among the strictly temperate.* This makes the number of deaths due to drink equal to one-fourth the total number of deaths among the hard drinkers. As the total number is 120,789, the number of these due to drink is 30,197. It is certain the number does not fall below this; it is almost certain that it should fall somewhat above it. Probably it will be safe to say that intemperance kills between 30,000 and 35,000 each year in England.

What is of more interest to us, however, is the number of deaths due to intemperance in America. If we take the number in England as a basis, and make allowance for the larger population in America, and the smaller consumption *per*

---

* The average age of the two classes, careless drinkers and inebriates, is 54.83 years, or 29.83 years after the 25th year, at which point the comparison begins. That of the temperate is 62.13, or 37.13 years after the 25th year, one-fourth longer.

caput, * we shall obtain the following figures for America:

Number hard drinkers in United States (male and female) over 25 years of age	2,480,000.
Number of deaths each year (from all causes) among the above	120,000
Number of these deaths due directly to drink	30,000.

In the number here given of deaths due to intemperance (30,000) the deaths are not included of infants and children, many of which are undoubtedly due, either by reason of negligence, cruelty, or transmitted defects, to the intemperance of parents. What this number is can only be conjectured, but there is no doubt it is considerable. It is not improbable, indeed, that the most destructive work of intemperance is among this class. Nor is the number included of those who die from intemperance before the age of 25. This however is very inconsiderable. It is not probable that many, even if they form confirmed habits of intemperance at an earlier age, die as the result of those habits before their twenty-fifth year.

As a result, then, of the investigations of the British Medical Association, we may say that out of a population, in the United States, Jany. 1, 1889, of sixty-five millions, there were nearly two and one-half millions of hard drinkers, one hundred and twenty thousand of whom die each year, and thirty thousand of whom owe their deaths directly to intemperance.

---

* By the report of the Swiss Federal Council, the consumption of alcohol in Great Britain in 1880 was 2.6787 gallons *per caput*; in the United States, 1.1329 gallons *per caput.*

10. The Economical Evils of Drink.

The second class of evils to be considered are the economical evils. These are evils that come home to all classes of society, but especially to the wage-earners. In fact, on this class all the economical burdens of society fall most heavily. The wage-earner has, in general, but one thing to sell—his labor—and that he must sell from day to day. If the price of labor is low, he can not, except in a very limited degree, hold back for a rise; if the price of labor is high, he can not sell more than when the price was low. If the burdens of taxation on the landlord are increased, he can in part relieve himself by shifting the burdens, or a portion of them, on his tenants; they in turn may shift all or a part, if they are manufacturers or merchants, on their customers, who in their turn may shift a portion upon the help they employ— the wage-earner. But the latter is not in a condition to shift his share of the burden. He can not dictate terms, as a rule, for he must sell his labor or in a short time starve, and he must buy the necessaries of life or come to the same point. It is not true that all economical burdens, at whatever point of society applied, rest finally on those at the bottom; the burdens are always distributed somewhat. But it is true that those burdens rest most heavily on those at the bottom, on the wage-earners. Punch's picture of the soldier who fights for all, the statesman who makes laws for all, the priest who prays for all, and the laborer *who pays for all,* is a *caricature* of the truth, but it is a caricature *of the truth.*

The moral evils of the liquor traffic are to a large extent borne by those who are to blame for them—by the drunkards themselves. But the economical evils are, for the most part, borne by those who are not to blame for them—by those indeed who are least to blame. The drunkard is an economical burden not to himself, nor to the saloon-keeper, but to the sober and the industrious. If he fails to work, he is a dead-weight on society. If he works, it is likely to be in a fitful uncertain manner that disorders industry and trade. Especially is this true in those forms of industry in which men work by twos and threes, when the drunkenness of one means the enforced idleness of others.

It has been urged at times that if all working men were sober the price of sober labor would go down as the supply increased. But such an objection is based on ignorance of the primary truths of social science. In organized society, under normal conditions, all labor properly expended creates more value than it consumes. Were it not for this, industry would prove a curse to a community, and the more industrious a community the more poverty-stricken it would become. On the contrary, in any industrious community wealth accumulates, and as it accumulates the demand for labor increases, for two reasons: namely, first, because by the accumulation of wealth labor can be applied to better advantage, and so as to produce more valuable results; and, second, because human nature is so constituted that the more its wants are supplied the more rapidly they increase. The family that want this year nothing but a log cabin to shelter them, when they get that, begin to want a dozen of things to make it comfortable and attractive—beds, chairs, tables, kitchen utensils, fuel, carpets. So in a community of families, the creation of wealth adds steadily to the number of wants and the demand for labor. Civilization has a thousand times as many calls for labor as barbarism.

If, therefore, in a community of one hundred families, fifty sober men work and fifty drunken men idle, the demand for labor next year will not be as great as it would have been had all one hundred labored this year. Each of the sober fifty bears a heavier burden because of the drunken fifty.

So far, then, from the value of sober labor's being increased by drunkenness, the reverse is true, and not only for the reason just given, but for another reason equally apparent. The drunkard *cheapens the labor market* in the same way that the dealer who sells books below cost cheapens and demoralizes the book market. The drunkard is ready to sell, not only his own labor, but that of his wife and children, at less than the real market value. The result is an irruption of woman-labor and child-labor at whatever price employers will pay.

While we are trying to bar out cheap labor from abroad, the saloon is steadly cheapening labor at home.

In attempting to reckon, in dollars and cents, the economical loss involved in a harmless luxury, such, for instance, as the use of jewelry, two values must be considered : (1) The intrinsic value of the material used ; (2) the value of the labor expended upon it. The diamond pin, for instance, represents (1) a withdrawal from useful purposes of the diamonds and the gold ; and (2) a withdrawal from useful purposes of all the labor that has been expended upon the pin. In these two values lies the economical loss involved in the pin, no matter whether its cost to the wearer was $100, or $1000. But in the case of harmful luxuries, there is another cost to be considered—the cost of damages.

In reckoning the cost to society of drink, three values must be considered : (1) The value of the materials used, such as grain and hops ; (2) the value of the labor that has been expended in producing the drink and marketing it ; (3) the value of whatever is destroyed or impaired by the drink, including loss of life, loss of work-power, expense involved in the arrest, trial, and punishment for crime, the care of paupers, insane, feeble-minded, and inebriates.

The first and second of these values can be readily computed. It is, for all practical purposes, equivalent to the drink-bill of the nation, less the taxes and fees paid out by the traffic into the public treasury. Suppose that $700,000,000 is the sum paid each year for drink in this country. Not a dollar of this sum, it may be, will be lost to the nation; but the labor and the material used in making and marketing the liquor for which this sum was expended, are lost to the nation. The value of that material and labor is represented by the $700,000,000 after the taxes and license fees are deducted.

Suppose, by way of illustration, that this nation withdraws from other forms of industry 500,000, men, and sends them to labor for one year in the construction of the Nicaragua canal. Let $700,000,000 be the sum paid them for their labor, their transportation, the cost of machinery, and all their appliances. And suppose, further, that in one way or another every dollar of this sum is by the end of the year returned again to the nation, either in exchange for provisions purchased, or in bank deposits, or in some other form. The nation would not have lost a single dollar of the $700,000,000, but it would have lost *the equivalent of that sum*, in the necessaries, comforts, and luxuries supplied to these men. If the work they have in the meantime performed has created a canal whose value is $700,000,000, the nation has lost nothing but interest. If the work has proved valueless, the loss has been $700,000,000 plus the interest. If the work has proved to be positively destructive, the amount of value destroyed must be added to the $700,000,000 to ascertain the full extent of the loss.

It has been estimated that 500,000 men are, in one way or other, engaged in this country in the making and marketing of liquor, and that $700,000,000 is the sum paid to them by the consumers. Not a dollar of this sum, it may be, is lost ; but the equivalent is lost, and, in addition, all the damage entailed is so much of a loss.

An estimate made in 1886 by Mr. Barrett, at the request of the Bureau of Statistics at Washington, and published in the Report of the Bureau, December, 1886, places the sum paid for liquor by the consumers of the nation at $700,000,000 a year. About the same time, and independently of Mr. Barrett's estimate, Edward Atkinson had figured out about the same result.* Others have estimated the drink-bill at a much higher figure, but none that the writer knows of has placed the figures lower. From this sum should be deducted the aggregate taxes and license fees paid by the traffic, under Federal, State or Municipal laws. The total receipts to the Federal Government during the year ending June 30, 1888, (see Report of Internal Revenue Dept. for that year) amounted to $69,306,166.41 on distilled liquors, and $23,324,218.48 on fermented liquors —a total of $92,630,384.89. From this is to be

---

* This estimate of Mr. Barrett's has been assailed by Mr. Thomann, of the U. S. Brewers' Association, but the only point he makes, of serious moment, is that from this sum, $700,000,000, should be deducted the taxes and fees paid into the public treasury by the traffic, in estimating the loss to the nation.

deducted the cost of collecting, which would reduce the sum to about $91,000,000. During the same year there were 176,748 retail and 7,185 wholesale dealers according to the report of the Internal Revenue Department. If we take $200 as the average license fee, the aggregate fees amounted to $36,800,000.* From this are to be deducted the costs of excise boards or collectors, bringing the sum down certainly as low as $33,-000,000. This makes a total of $124,000,000 to be deducted from $700,000,000, leaving $576,-000,000 as the approximate direct cost each year of the liquor traffic,—about $9.00 *per caput*, or $45.00 per family.

In addition must be considered the cost of damages inflicted by the traffic, in the way of crimes engendered, work-power lost, etc. The first item under this head will be the loss of 30,000 lives, not counting the infants and children whose deaths are due to intemperance of parents. If each of these lives be reckoned at an industrial value of $1000 (not an unusual price paid for an able-bodied slave before the war) we have $30,000,000 as the amount of this item. (Here it may be urged that the death of a drunkard, so far from being an industrial loss, is a positive gain. That is so; but the fact of his being a drunkard instead of an able-bodied man, is due to drink, and his industrial

---

* Since writing this, the writer finds that Mr. Thomann also estimates $200 as the average license fee, in his pamphlet : "The Nation's Drink-bill Economically Considered." p. 18. No exact estimate is possible. License fees range from $30 to $1000 in different parts of the country.

value, not as he was just prior to death, but as he would have been but for drink, is the value to be considered.) Another item is the loss of productive power on the part of 2,500,000 intemperate drinkers. A large proportion of these consist of persons who have never learned any trade or profession, and whose labor, being unskilled, is not so much impaired by drink. Another large proportion consists of those who would, under any circumstances, either with or without drink, be idlers and vagabonds. On the other hand, the loss of a days' work will in many cases, where men work in twos or threes, as in iron mills and in mines, cause the loss of work on the part of others. Altogether a loss of ten per cent. in the productive capacity of these 2,500,000 hard drinkers, as due to drink, seems to be a very moderate estimate.* Counting three hundred working days to the year at an average of $1.50 per day, one-tenth of the productive capacity of 2,500,000 adults would be $112,500,000, as another loss due to drink.

---

* In the report of the Secretary of the Board of State Charities of Massachusetts for 1868 (Pub. Doc. 17 p. 34), testimony is cited from a large manufacturing house in North Easton, Mass., namely Oliver Ames & Son, to the following effect:

"We have over 400 men in our works here. We find that the present license law has a very bad effect among our employees. We find on comparing our production in May and June of this year (1868) with that of the corresponding months of last year (1867) that in 1867, with 375 men, we produced (8) eight per cent. more goods than we did in the same months in 1868 with 400 men. We attribute this falling off entirely to the repeal of the prohibitory law and the great increase in the use of intoxicating liquors among our men in consequence."

In a report made by the Commission appointed by the Canadian Government in 1874 "to inquire into the working of the prohibitory "liquor law" in the United States, "the following testimony is given (p. 65) from H. Wilson, woollen manufacturer of Southboro, Mass:

During 1868, the year the license law was in force, our cost of production was nearly 10 per cent. more. I employed about 150 men and the drinking by some of them interfered with all, and diminished production, but not cost."

Another considerable item is the cost of crimes due to drink, the care of the paupers and demented whose condition is due to drink, and the damages by fire, by rail, by boat, and in other ways, due to drunken carelessness or recklessness. By the additions made in the items already reckoned the direct cost $576,000,000, has been increased to $718,500,000. What this last item would amount to it is impossible to tell. But it is reasonably certain it would bring the sum total somewhere between eight and nine hundred millions of dollars as the yearly cost, direct and indirect, of drink.*

There are many who will assail this estimate as far too low. Other estimates have been made that placed the cost of drink more than twice as high. But this has been done by counting in not only the actual money expended for drink, but, beside, the value of the labor and material used in the various forms of the traffic,—thus just doubling the proper figures. Frequently, too, the number of lives lost by drink is placed from 60,000 to 100,000, for which the writer is unable to find any but the most flimsy basis. From the nature of the case, no estimate can be exact. The most that can be done is to give a general idea of the magnitude of the evil. The endeavor has been,

---

* In a work on "Our Penal Machinery and Its Victims," by J. P. Altgeld, of Chicago, in 1884, it was estimated that the total arrests for all causes number in the nation 2,500,000 each year; that the cost of police is on an average $24.00 to each arrest; that the cost of the 50 large penitentiaries, the 2200 jails, and numerous police prisons, is at least $400,000,000, interest on which at five per cent. would be $20,000,000. Then there is, in addition, the cost of keeping prisoners over and above the value of the work they perform.

in the preceding pages, not to see how large the figures could be made, but to keep the estimates within those limits in which we have satisfactory data for our guidance.

11. Political Evils Due to the Saloon.

The third form of evil attendant on the drink traffic, is the political evil.

The saloon as a factor in politics has, of late years, drawn to it the attention of the nation. Whether it be true that the influence of the saloon-keeper is, as Judge Rhone thinks, "im-"mensely overated," is not the question of greatest importance. The influence of *the saloon*, rather than the influence of the saloon-keeper, is the cause of grave concern. The influence of the saloons of the land is no more to be measured by that of the men who conduct them than the influence of the common schools of the land is to be measured by that of the teachers employed in them. The bar rather than the barkeeper is the source of degradation, and if every saloon-keeper emigrated or died to-morrow, and the saloons continued, there would be but a slight and temporary change for the better. It is true the liquor-dealers, through the organizations—local, state, and national—which they have formed, and the immense capital which they have accumulated, have developed political power dangerous to contemplate. But the chief source of that power is not, after all, in their organizations, nor in their capital, nor in their personal ability; but it lies in the saloons which they control, and through which they operate to such tremendous advantage. Whatever purchasable vote there may be, is almost sure to be within reach of the saloon-keeper. If each saloon of New York State can reach and control ten votes on an average, the united strength of the 35,000 saloons is one-fourth of the vote of the State.

Nor is this one of the mere might-be evils which sometimes give needless nightmares to reformers. The power is one which is exercised already, not indeed as a unified force, but sufficiently to determine important elections. In the last election (1888) the Democratic candidate for President, with the Independent vote largely in his favor, polled in New York State 635,757 votes. The vote polled the same day for the Democratic candidate for Governor, though the Independent vote was almost solidly cast against him, was 650,464. The former was defeated by 13,000 plurality, the latter elected by 19,000 plurality. The difference, it is generally conceded, was brought about by the liquor dealers, who believed the re-election of the Democratic candidate for Governor was important for their interests.

If, as is probable, 15,000 of the votes cast for the Democratic candidate for President were cast against the Democratic candidate for Governor, then there must have been at least 30,000 who cast their votes for the Republican candidate for President, who were swung over the same day to the support of the Democratic candidate for Governor. A study of the returns shows that this transference took place chiefly in the cities, confirming the general opinion that it was effected by the liquor dealers. A similar swing in the other direction was witnessed in 1883, when the Republican candidate for Secretary of State in New York was regarded by the liquor dealers with special favor, and the Democratic candidate was regarded with special disfavor. The former was elected by 18,583 plurality, while every other candidate on the same ticket was defeated by pluralities ranging from 13,630 to 17,568.

These are instances of what has appeared in the more general elections. But it is in the less conspicuous elections that the saloon plays the most important part. In the elections for the Legislature, county and municipal offices, the saloon is, in the centres of population, too often the dominant force. It is here that it plays its most dangerous because least conspicuous role. The politicians whom it breeds are, as a rule, men whose ambitions are directed to local offices, and whose only interest in the general elections is in the occasion they present for "deals." The notorious Board of "Boodle" Aldermen in power in New York city in 1884, contained twelve liquor dealers, or ex-dealers, out of a total membership of twenty-four, and the Board that succeeded to power was similarly constituted. With the right vested, as it was at that time, in the Board to confirm or reject all the Mayor's appointments to office, it will be seen what such power meant to the city of New York. Out of 1002 primaries and nominating conventions held in New York in 1884 by the two leading parties, 633 were held in saloons, and 96 in rooms adjacent to saloons. (New York City and its Masters, p. 38.) In 1887 the County Committee of one of the two leading parties in New York, and that the one considered less amenable to saloon influences, contained fifty-three liquor dealers, or ex-dealers, the ratio of liquor dealers being larger than that of any other profession or trade. Similar instances might be given showing much the same condition of things in Brooklyn, Boston, Cincinnati, Chicago, St. Louis, Omaha, Baltimore, San Francisco, and other large cities of the Union, in all of which it is true, to greater or less degree, that, as Mr. Halstead said of Cincinnati, "every saloon is a politi- "cal club house." "Long ago," said George Frederic Parsons in *The Atlantic Monthly*, two years since, "the saloon abolished party politics in " our largest cities. To-day, in every such city, " the local government is vested in neither party, " but is in the hands of the saloon itself. Nom- " inally, the government may be Democratic or " Republican. Actually, it is in commission by a " band of venal politicians, who have no convic- " tions or principles, who trade and swap oppor- " tunities for plunder with one another, who act "as agents for the so-called party leaders, but who acknowledge allegiance only to the saloon."

As a result of this political prominence of the saloon, is seen the municipal misrule which is generally recognized by statesmen at home and abroad, as the most glaring defect of American Government, and the most ominous danger to its perpetuity. "There is no denying," says Prof. Bryce in his new and valuable work "The American Commonwealth," "that the government of cities is the one conspicuous failure of the United States." Yet municipal government has come to be the most important part of American Government. The massing of our population in the large cities has been going on in steadily increasing proportions, until now more than one-fifth of the population of the United States is contained in the fifty largest cities. Not only the balance of power but the power itself, politically and financially, has been fast coming to these great nerve-centres of the nation, where social customs are set, public sentiment moulded, and the lines of industrial and commercial activity determined. Rottenness here is rottenness at the core. De Tocqueville forty years ago pointed out our danger through municipal misrule; Beaconsfield and Macaulay have emphasized it since. It is in the large cities that the saloon is strongest and most defiant. It is here that its mastery in politics is most complete and most offensive; and it is here also that the Church and the influences which make for morality are relatively the weakest. The sober truth is, the saloon has seized upon the strategic points of American civilization—the cities—and, in so far as local government is concerned, it has obtained a grip that only the sternest measures can break.

There have been, during the last half-century, several outbreaks of public sentiment awakened by the rapid increase of our foreign population. Unfortunately, these outbreaks have seemed to be directed against persons rather than against ideas or influences. The cry has been, " America for Americans," rather than, America for American ideas and institutions. The distinction is one with a difference. There are legions of foreign-born citizens who are to-day *Americans* in all that that word implies. In many cases their love for this country and its institutions is more intelligent and more appreciative from the very fact of their birth under other skies. The danger lies not with the foreign-born citizen so much as with the foreign-born ideas, customs, and standards to which too often he persists in clinging.

It is a duty that is owed not to the native-born American alone, but equally to the foreign-born, that those influences which have hitherto made this land an asylum for all peoples should continue to dominate in the future development of the nation. " We are placed at the head of rep-" resentative and popular governments," said Webster in his Bunker Hill oration. " We shall "be recreant to the duty of that headship if we "permit the fundamental conditions of national "repose, of the security of personal rights, of good "laws, and of just administration to be imperilled "by the ignorant, lawless, idle, and dangerous "overflow of all other countries. We are the "occupants and guardians of this country, "and with a kindly heart and hospitable hand "toward all the world, we must prescribe the "conditions upon which the world shall come "here."

Closing the ports, however, on those whose only offence has been birth in a foreign land, so far from being a blow struck for American ideas, is a direct blow at one of the most cherished of those ideas, and one which has done much to keep the patriotic pride of the nation alive. Such a measure could be justified by the direst necessity alone, and after all other measures had proved futile. No reference is intended in this to the laws against imported paupers and criminals, nor to the intent of the law against contract labor. It is not the man that *is brought* here, but the one who of his own will, aspiring for better things for himself or his children, with thrift enough to pay for his passage and courage enough to brave the hardships of the new life—to withdraw from such an one our welcome would mark a grave departure from the spirit of American history. There has been, of course, a great deal of spread-eagle oratory that counted for very little about our country as the asylum for the oppressed of all lands. But below all the buncombe and braggadocio, there has been a deep-seated pride in the fact and a glorying in it that has stimulated the patriotism of the nation to a wonderful degree.

And yet, while appreciating this to the full, one must not fail to recognize the perils that have come with the foreignizing tendencies of the last two decades. The advance of science has in the last forty years annihilated ten out of every twelve miles that separate us from the old world. It is as if our continent had been taken up in the hand of Omnipotence and placed within one-sixth of its former distance from the nations of Europe. The change has brought to us wonderful development and marvelous wealth, but it has brought its dangers as well. The number of immigrants reaching our ports in the last twenty years has exceeded the sum total of immigration during the entire previous history of our nation. One thousand and five hundred a day has been about the average for the last ten years, and the massing of these in the large cities has greatly complicated the problems arising. " When an Irishman, a Ger-" man, a Frenchman, lands at Castle Garden," says Sam Small, " then and there an Irishman, a " German, or a Frenchman ought to die, and an " American be born." But unfortunately such a transformation is becoming more and more rare. We have the German vote and the Irish vote. In each of the large cities there is the German quarter, the Irish quarter, the Italian quarter. Natural enough, of course, but dangerous enough too. It is perhaps not too much to say that the central question of our social and political future for years to come will be this:

SHALL AMERICA AMERICANIZE THIS VAST FOREIGN ELEMENT, OR BE FOREIGNIZED BY IT?

The bearing which the saloon has upon this question is immediate and important, and more so in a political than any other sense. Itself an imported institution, the saloon has become the fulcrum by means of which the worst of the foreignizing tendencies work their changes on law and Government. It is linked in an alliance with the house of prostitution, which is already seeking *and finding* legalization in the form of license laws. More than any other one factor, the saloon has broken down the American Sabbath and ushered in the Continental Sunday, disdaining in most cases even to change the law, but accomplishing its work in spite of the law.* It is in the saloon that Anarchism finds a rendezvous and an inspiration, and the red flag has never floated to the American breeze except from an American saloon.

But above and beyond all, the saloon has organized and in a large part *created* a purchasable vote whose proportions have alarmed even American

---

* Out of 3441 applicants to the License Court of Philadelphia, in 1838, for saloon licenses, 3000 were reported by the police as violators of the Sunday law.

optimism. If "every saloon is a political club-"house," the education given in it is an education in political corruption. As a rule, every habitual drunkard added to society is an addition of one to the purchasable vote. Said John B. Finch in his impassioned way:

"There stands a workman; he does not drink; he has money in his pocket; he has a good job; his brain is clear; his wife and family are happy. For the first time he goes to a drinking place and drinks. During four or five years he goes down and down, and by and by he gets reckless, loses his business, and his family have to beg. He is an outcast on the street. On an election morning this man stands on a street corner, ragged, dirty, sick; craving for something to drink, such a craving for the poison that he would sell his soul for a drink of liquor. The only thing that man possesses which will bring money is his vote. Do you suppose that man, with morals gone, reputation gone, starving, ragged, and hungry, will vote like an American citizen, according to his convictions, if he can get money for voting otherwise?"—(*The People vs The Liquor Traffic. p.* 58.)

It is in the saloon, and under its corrupting influences, that the immigrant, as a rule, learns his first lessons in American politics. Within a radius of one-half mile from Castle Garden four hundred saloons are located, and up to a very recent date there was not in that distance a lodging house or restaurant without a bar attached. Who is to blame if political corruption, as a lucrative business and a speedy channel to official power, is learned by the immigrant too well ever to be unlearned? In the city of Philadelphia, in 1888, the License Court began a system of inquiry into the nationality of the applicants for license. It was found that nine out of ten were of foreign birth, and a large percentage were still unnaturalized. A similar condition of things doubtless exists in other large cities, and in some of them, probably, the proportion of foreign-born saloon-keepers is larger still. George Frederic Parsons, in the article in " The Atlantic Monthly " already quoted, writes:

"The foreigner who lands in this country obtains his first ideas of its governmental system from the saloon. There he is introduced to the lowest intrigues of factional conflict. There he is taught that the chief end and aim of politics is to make as much as possible for the 'workers'. There he is enlisted into one or other of the great organizations which have reduced party politics to periodical battles for plunder, to contests for the opportunity to misgovern. There he learns that honor and principle are simply 'molasses to catch flies,' as a notorious politician once expressed it. There he is made to understand that he is not expected to think for himself, but that he must obey implicitly the party mandates, reverence the saloon-keepers of his ward, submit himself humbly to his 'boss,' and on election day be thankful that he can sell his vote for a couple of dollars or a debauch on bad whiskey. This is no fanciful picture. There is no considerable city in the United States in which purchased votes are not cast by the thousand at every important election, and these votes are almost invariably bought and paid for in the saloon."

It is, after all, in this aspect of the saloon, as a creator and a rallying point of corrupt forces in politics, that we have most to fear. It is this that makes the saloon a barrier to every reform that must appeal to the integrity and intelligence of the citizen for success. It is this above all that makes the drink question one that lies, as Cobden said, "at the foundation of all social and political "reform."

Ballot Reform bills may prove a check to the spread of this corruption in one direction; but Ballot Reform itself must now come, it seems, if it comes at all, modified at the dictates of saloon-bred politicians. But should it accomplish all it promises, it will reach but one phase of an all-pervading disease. It is not corruption at the ballot-box alone, but corruption in the primaries and nominating conventions, and corruption in office as well. In a magazine article a few years ago Mr. Theodore Roosevelt told of his experience in Albany as a legislator. When seeking to secure the passage of certain reform bills, he and his colleagues investigated with care the character of their fellow members of the legislature, with a view to finding out how many they could depend on to resist efforts at bribery. The conclusion they reached was that fully sixty per cent. of the legislators could not be relied on. Within the last few months, the President of the United States in his inaugural address, and a majority of the Governors, in their messages to the legislatures, have called attention to the extent of political corruption as one of the most serious and imminent dangers to the Commonwealth. It is fast becoming literally true that, as Wendell Phillips once said: "Universal suffrage is a sham while rum "rules our great cities."

12. The Pleasures of Drink.

Such are the evils, in outline, that are attendant upon the saloon. They are *public* evils, and justify whatever public action seems to be necessary for their prevention. That they are inseparable from the traffic, uniform experience indicates. What are the benefits which the traffic confers as an offset to these evils? In considering these, the plea made for liquor as a medicinal agent is, of course, not pertinent, since it is not proposed to abridge the manufacture or sale of liquor for medicinal, mechanical, or chemical purposes.

The plea is sometimes advanced that the traffic gives employment to many thousands of men and support to their families. This is true; but unless for that support some adequate return is made society, then their support is at the expense of others, and the larger the number employed in the traffic the greater becomes the economical evil. It is, moreover, a demonstrable fact that whereas one million dollars of capital invested in the manufacture of liquor gives employment to 285 persons, the same amount invested in one of the other ten leading industries of the nation gives employment, on an average, to 876 persons.* If the money, therefore, now invested in the manufacture of liquor were invested in other forms of industry it would give employment to three times as many men and pay two and one-half times as much as now in wages.

A similar plea to the above is often heard, to the effect that the liquor traffic furnishes to the farmer a valuable market for his grain. This plea is, when analyzed, equally as unsubstantial as the preceding one. The amount of corn, rye, and barley used in the manufacture of liquor is probably about one bushel out of every twenty raised by the farmer. But it must be evident that a very considerable proportion of the money now paid into the saloons would, but for drink, be expended in provisions, clothing, and similar necessities and comforts of life. For every dollar now expended for drink, the farmer receives about five cents for the grain furnished by him. For the same amount

---

*This estimate is based on the figures given in the Census Report for 1880.

of money expended in food-products, such for instance as bread, the farmer receives about seventeen cents out of every dollar.

After all is said, there remains but one plea that can be made for the traffic on the basis of any benefits it confers, and that is a plea for the social and physical pleasures derived from drink. Consideration is called to the fact that for every person who drinks to his ruin, there are many who derive a keen delight from drink without demonstrably impairing their faculties or rendering themselves burdens upon society.

It is not a slight thing to curtail the pleasures of mankind. In the divine plan, pleasures and pains seem to be the great forces, acting in opposite directions, which are bringing the race into conformity with the laws of nature and the purposes of the Creator. In the pleasure of possession as well as in the pains of poverty, are found the incentives to thrift and endeavor. The pleasures of health as well as the pains of disease are incentives to self-control and physical activity. The destruction of a legitimate pleasure is a positive *moral* loss to the world, and no nature can be anything but dwarfed in which the faculty of enjoyment has not been developed.

Were the question (as it is so often conceived to be) simply that of curtailing the enjoyments of the many to save a few from their self-inflicted pains, the objections to such a course would be numerous and strong. But the question is one radically different from that. Not to release the slave of appetite from the degradation which he has wrought upon himself, but to protect the Commonwealth from the burdens laid upon it by drink, and to protect the innocent and helpless victims of others' appetites, who are unable to protect themselves, is the prime purpose of prohibitory law.

For above and beyond all the evils that can be shown by statistics or figured into dollars and cents, are the heartbreaks of those who are linked to the drunkard by bonds indissoluble. It has been said that "there is no argument in a woman's "cry." Be that as it may, it is more than an argument: it is an appeal. A serious thing it may be to curtail the pleasures of mankind; but is it not far more serious to continue pleasures that can be had only by the continuance of conditions that are certain, ever and everywhere, to entail upon countless thousands woes that are immeasurable? The issue is not the wine-cup about which poets have sung, but the saloon, whose horrors only a Dante could fittingly describe.

If the preceding calculations are correct, the number of intemperate drinkers in our nation, and those who drink hard and constantly, is about 2,500,000. These represent, on the usual average, 10,000,000 others who are bound to them by family ties and to greater or less extent dependent upon them for support and protection. If, then, one-half the entire adult population of the nation are temperate drinkers, there is still, for every one who safely tastes the pleasures of drink, one to whom drink has brought sorrow, shame, and suffering that beggar description. Is such a pleasure worth a price so great?

13. Recapitulation.

In the preceding pages, the endeavor has been to set forth the following points:

1. That Prohibition is an established *legal* right of the Commonwealth.

2. That it is in harmony with those views of government on which social philosophers of all schools are agreed.

3. That its purpose is not to reform the moral conduct of the individual, but to relieve society of the burdens and dangers imposed upon it by drink.

4. That it interferes with the performance of no religious duty and does not involve a decision on the biblical questions that arise.

5. That instead of depriving the physician of full freedom in administering liquor as a medicine, it vindicates his right alone to decide when its medicinal use is demanded.

6. That the traffic in drink is attended by evils of exceptional gravity which are inseparable from it, and which are in no wise limited to those who participate in the traffic. That these evils are of three kinds: (1) Moral evils, including two-thirds of the criminal offenses, and the loss of thirty thousand lives each year; (2) economical evils,

aggregating a cost of between eight and nine hundred millions of dollars each year; (3) political evils that have a vital bearing on the most important political questions of the day.

7. That the pleasures conferred by the traffic are in striking disproportion to the evils it inflicts.

There still remain to be considered the questions, Does Prohibition work well in practice, and, Is a new party necessary or advisable for securing it?

PART II : THE POLICY.

IS THE POLICY OF PROHIBITION ONE WHICH, IN ACTUAL OPERATION, ACCOMPLISHES THE DESIRED ENDS?

"The man who writes, speaks, or meditates without being well-stocked with facts, as landmarks to the understanding, is like a mariner who sails along a treacherous coast without a pilot, or one who adventures in the wide ocean without a rudder or compass."—*Lord Bacon.*

"ARGUMENT however admirable, and logic however conclusive," wrote George William Curtis recently in dealing with another subject, "do not avail with the English-speaking race like actual experiment." Concerning any proposed public policy, the question asked by the social philosopher is, Is the principle embodied in the policy a correct one? The question asked by the politician is, Will the policy work? The statesman, with an eye both to ultimate tendencies and immediate results, is forced to ask both questions. Not until social science shall have become one of the exact sciences, can a nation afford to take more than a step at a time in untried paths, however many the attractions they present. Philosophy, after all, is but the deduction of general laws from the experiences of the past; and in social philosophy especially, the advent of a new fact or a new force, or a set of new experiences, may at times act upon the best of theories much as the advent of a new planet in our solar system might act upon the calculations of our astronomers.

Fortunately for the consideration of the subject of this volume, the experiments with prohibitory legislation have already lasted for more than a generation and have been tried under many different conditions.

There are at present five States of the Union— namely, Maine, Vermont, Rhode Island, Kansas, and Iowa—under prohibitory law which applies, in each case, to the entire State. In New Hampshire there is Prohibition of the sale but not of the manufacture of liquor. In addition to these States, prohibitory law applying to the entire State has been on the statute books of three other States, namely, Massachusetts, Connecticut, and Michigan. In addition still to these, portions more or less considerable of many other States are now under prohibitory law secured by county or municipal action, those States in which these portions are most considerable being: Georgia, Mississippi, Tennessee, Kentucky, North Carolina, South Carolina, Arkansas, Massachusetts, and Connecticut. In nearly all the States, however, there is, as in New York, Illinois, Ohio, and Nebraska, local Prohibition to some extent.

In two of the five States now under the operation of State Prohibiton, the law has had an almost continuous existence for more than thirty years—namely, Maine and Vermont. In Rhode Island the present law was adopted in May 1886, but prior to that time, namely, from 1853 to 1862, and again from 1874 to 1875, Rhode Island was under statutory Prohibition. In Kansas and Iowa the law has been in existence respectively eight and four years. In three of the five States, namely, Maine, Kansas and Rhode Island, the law has been imbedded in the State Constitution.

In addition, a number of other States, during the period from 1851–1855, adopted prohibitory laws, through the action of the Legislature, which were either declared unconstitutional by reason of certain clauses confiscating liquor in the market prior to the passage of the law, or which were repealed in a very short time before the machinery for their execution could be constructed or fairly tried. As interest centres chiefly in the five States now under the operation of the law, the examination into the results in those States formerly under prohibitory laws, which have since been repealed, will not be made in elaborate detail. These States number four, namely, Michigan, Rhode Island, Connecticut, and Massachusetts.

In three of these four States, namely, Michigan, Rhode Island and Massachusetts, the law was adopted in the same year—1855. In the other State, Connecticut, the law was adopted the year previous. One highly important consideration presents itself at once, from these dates of enactment, and that is, the political condition of the country at this time or immediately thereafter. The question of African slavery was rapidly becoming the all-absorbing question of the nation. The Republican party had just had its birth (1854), on the issue of the non-extension of slavery, polling in its first national campaign, two years later (so intense had the feeling already become) one and one-third millions of votes. The Whig party was being broken in pieces, in the South by the Know-Nothings, in the North by the Republicans. In Congress a struggle was going on that absorbed the attention of the Nation as never before or since. The very atmosphere grew electric with excitement and nowhere more so than in the three New England States we are considering. The existence of the Union was hanging in the balance. Civil war followed soon, in 1861, lasting until 1866.

In the second year of the war, the prohibitory law was repealed in Rhode Island, and superseded by a license law, the need for increased revenue being doubtless at that time an important factor in bringing about the change. The law was re-enacted in 1874, but its trial then was limited to a single year.

In Massachusetts the prohibitory provisions of the law were repealed the second year after the war closed (1867); two years later (early in 1870) these provisions were re-enacted, but in the same year malt liquor was exempted from the prohibition. Three years later, this exemption was withdrawn, and two years later still (1875) the entire law was superseded by a license law.

In Michigan, the law remained on the statute-books until 1875, but prior to that, a decision had been made by the State Supreme Court, giving to municipalities the right, under the law, of taxing the traffic, which effectually disposed of what force the law had possessed.

In Connecticut, the law continued in force until 1872, when it was superseded by license and local option.

It becomes evident, then, that in each of these four States, for at least ten years immediately succeeding the enactment of Prohibition, the excitement leading up to and during the war rendered the conditions unfavorable to a concentration of either attention or energy upon its enforcement. Even in local elections the issue of slavery had become dominant and dividing, and, as a matter of fact, the enforcement of Prohibition seems during this period to have been a matter of very little political moment.

1. The Inquiry Instituted by the Canadian Parliament.

It is fortunate for the investigation at this point, that in 1874 the Governor-General of Canada, at the solicitation of the Canadian Parliament, appointed a Special Commission " to inquire into "the working of the prohibitory liquor laws." This commission consisted of two men, namely, F. Davis, a lawyer, and Rev. J. M. Manning. They seem to have investigated with much painstaking the effects of the law in Maine and Massachusetts, and, less thoroughly, the effects in Vermont, Michigan, Connecticut, and Rhode Island. The results of their investigation were embodied in a report to the Secretary of State of Canada, printed in 1875. Taking up their report as it pertains to the four States now under consideration, namely, Michigan, Rhode Island, Connecticut, and Massachusetts, we find the condition of things in each of those States to have been as follows :

Michigan. It seems to have been generally admitted that the law in this State was not enforced to any appreciable extent, except in some of the rural communities. "In all the large cities and "towns," Governor Bagley wrote to the Commission, "the law was inoperative and not enforced "at all." Rev. John Russell, "the father of Prohi-"bition in Michigan," wrote to the Commission to the same effect, saying, "the prohibitory clauses "of the law were not generally enforced." Yet the law itself, in this State, was, according to the judgment of the Commission, "the best prohibi-"tory law" they found anywhere. The reasons for its non-enforcement are not pointed out. It was doubtless due to the twin causes of public indifference and official apathy.

Rhode Island. The report of the Commission gives but little of fact in regard to the results in this State during the period from 1854 to 1862. A letter is quoted from Hon. W. R. Watson, Secretary of State, written in 1854, in which emphatic testimony was given as to the good results of the law, but the letter gives only general statements, not specific facts, such as : " Its "effect, I cannot doubt, has been greatly to "diminish crime, pauperism, insanity, and that "long dark catalogue of evils—moral, social and "physical—which result from intemperance." Something more specific than this is given by the Commission for the year 1852, during which the State was under a prohibitory law which was soon pronounced unconstitutional. The figures given for Providence county show a reduction in the number of committals to the county jail, from 161 in the license year of 1851, to 99 in the prohibitory year of 1852 ; and a reduction in the number of committals for drunkenness in the city of Providence, from 282 in three months of 1851, to 177 in the corresponding three months of 1852. The conclusion drawn by the Commission in reference to this State is probably safe enough as far as it goes, namely, that the law was "in some parts of the "State well enforced, in others not." (p. 49.)

Connecticut. In this State, according to the annual messages of Governor Dutton and Governor Minor, in 1855 and 1856 respectively, the law was well enforced in those years and its benefits were marked. Governor Dutton said, as quoted by the Commission (p. 78.) : "There is "scarcely an open grog-shop in the State, the jails "are fast becoming tenantless, and a delightful "air of security is everywhere enjoyed." Governor Minor's statements are to a similar effect, as are also those quoted from Dr. Leonard Bacon, then and now a sturdy opponent of Prohibition. Dr. Bacon said : " * * * * its [the "law's] effect in promoting peace, order, quiet, "and general prosperity no man can deny. Never "for twenty years has our city [New Haven] "been so quiet as under its action." These testimonies, it will be noticed, refer entirely to the first two years after the law was enacted. (Dr. Bacon afterward testified before the Joint Special Committee of the Massachusetts Legislature, that the year after his testimony just quoted was given, the political control of the city passed into the hands of a party hostile to the law, and the good effects of Prohibition soon disappeared.) The only facts given by the Commission for later years were the number of jail committals in the State for the prohibitory year 1866, and for the two years (1873-4) following the law's repeal. In 1866 the number of commitments is given as 1576* ; in the year ending March, 1873 (partly a license and partly a prohibitory year), they num-

---

* This is the number given in the Report of the Commission. Official figures for that year give the number as 1827. For the other years, 1873-4, the figures given by the Commission agree with the official figures.

bered 2985; in the year ending March 1874 (wholly a license year) they numbered 4481. (Complete official figures will be found in Appendix, note D, showing the number of commitments in Connecticut for the entire period under Prohibition—1854-1873, as well as under license—1873-1884).

Massachusettes. In this State the Commission seem to have investigated results with more care than was bestowed upon any other State. The evidence obtained was of two kinds, the opinions of public men, and official statistics. Nearly all this evidence, however, pertains to the period immediately following the close of the Civil war. It seems to have been generally understood that for the period of 1856-1866 the enforcement of the law was not at all general. " For ten years it was "a dead letter act," is the statement made to the Commission by Captain Boynton, chief of the State Police.

In the year 1867, however, a vigorous effort was made for the enforcement of the law, through a State constabulary appointed for that special purpose. This enforcement led to a combined assault upon the law by all its opponents, which resulted in its repeal November, 1867, the new regime of license lasting until 1869. The comparisons between 1867 and 1868, one a prohibitory and one a license year, are furnished by the Commission's report as follows :

The commitments to the Massachusettes State

prison, which in the first nine months of 1866, a year of unenforced Prohibition, had numbered 156, fell in the first nine months of the year following, under the vigorous efforts to enforce the law, to 80. In the next year (1868) under license, they numbered, for the corresponding nine months, 143. (The figures are given for nine months of each year, instead of twelve, because the prohibitory law was in force but nine months of 1867.) The inspectors of the State prison, in their official report, attribute this increase in commitments in 1868 to the repeal of the prohibitory law.

In the city of Boston, where the efforts to enforce the law in 1867 were less successful than anywhere else in the State, the reports of the Chief of Police show nevertheless an increase in the cases of drunk and disorderly, from 6690 for the last six months of 1867 (which includes two months after the repeal of Prohibition*) to 8053 in the corresponding months of 1868. In addition to this increase, the record showed an increase of 3838 in the number of station-house lodgers (vagrants), and an increase of 248 in the number of criminal arrests. The following shows the total increase:

```
Increase of criminal arrests...................................................... 248
Increase of station-house lodgers............................................. 3838
Increase of drunkenness and assaults ...................................... 1363
    Increase for the six months under the license system .......... 5,449
```

In addition to this increase, there was an in-

---

* The license law did not, legally, go into effect until 1868, but practically the prohibitory law became inoperative with the election of November, 1867.

crease during the same period of six months of "not far from twenty-five per cent." to "the vari-"ous correctional and pauper institutions of Suf-"folk county."

A still fuller comparison was made in the Report of the Board of State Charities, in 1868. In most cases, under the prohibitory law, the drunkard was punished with a fine only; when the fine could not be paid, the offender was sent to Jail, to the House of Correction, or to the House of Industry. The number of such commitments increased in the entire State from 2501 in six months of 1867 (April—October) to 3170 in the corresponding six months of 1868.

The Governor of the State (Governor Claflin), the State Constable, the Board of Inspectors of the State Prison, and the Board of State Charities, all called attention, in very emphatic language, to this increase of crime, and *all, without exception, attributed it to the repeal of the prohibitory law.* In consequence of this increase of crime Prohibition was re-enacted, going again into force January, 1870, but in the same year additional legislation was enacted exempting malt liquors from the provisions of the law. The figures indicate but a slight decrease of crime during the following years. From the fall of 1873 to the fall of 1874, there was another year of complete prohibitory law, the enforcement of which seems to have attained a fair degree of efficiency toward the close of the year, when again, as in 1867, the enemies of the law rallied at the polls and elected a license legislature, by which license and local option laws were enacted in 1875, which are still in force.

In the foregoing brief resumè, little reference has been made to other evidence than that embodied in the report of the Canadian Commissioners. Importance is attached to that report for two reasons: (1) Because it embodies the result of an official investigation made soon after the trial of Prohibition in these States had come to an end, and while facts were fresh in the minds of men regarding it; (2) Because this investigation was conducted by officials from a neighboring kingdom, who, it is to be presumed, were entirely free from either political or personal entanglements that might have biased their minds. The evidence adduced by this Commission was obtained by personal visitation to the States mentioned, and communication, either orally or by letter, with those whose testimonies are given.

Other evidence confirms the general character of this report. In 1867 a Joint Special Committee was appointed by the Massachusetts Legislature to investigate the effects of the prohibitory law in that State. The committee held twenty-seven sittings in Boston, early in 1867, and examined 108 witnesses summoned by those opposing the prohibitory law, 75 witnesses summoned by the friends of the law, and 9 witnesses from the College of Pharmacy who had petitioned for a repeal of the law. Among these witnesses were ex-Governors, constables, sheriffs, judges, attorneys, city missionaries, mayors, chiefs of police, college professors, ministers, physicians, manufacturers and others. The testimony of each is given in the Report of the Committee, which is published in a large octavo volume of 898 pages. The testimonies given by eminent men in regard to the effects of the prohibitory law were so divergent, that the only conclusion to be drawn is that the effects of the law (prior to 1867) had been equally divergent in different portions of the State. As an almost invariable rule, however, those known as temperance men expressed themselves emphatically in favor of the law, while with few exceptions the witnesses summoned by the opponents of the law acknowledged their habits of drinking. As a result of this investigation, eight of the committee signed a report in favor of the repeal of the law and six signed reports in favor of its continuance.

The figures showing the commitments to Jail in Connecticut for each year from 1852 to 1872 (the period of Prohibition), and from 1872 to 1884 (a period of license,) have been compiled with much care by E. P. Augur, of Middletown, Conn., (see Appendix, note D.), from official returns and jail records. These figures show, despite the lax enforcement of the prohibitory law, a marked increase of crime immediately upon the repeal of the law. Taking the commitments to Jail during the years of Prohibition following the war, namely, 1866–1872, inclusive, and the first seven years following its repeal, and we have the following:

SEVEN YEARS UNDER PROHIBITORY LAW.		SEVEN YEARS OF LICENSE AND LOCAL OPTION.	
1866	1827	1873	4481
1867	1693	1874	4448
1868	1821	1875	4425
1869	2246	*1876	3103
1870	2593	1877	4149
1871	2805	1878	4577
1872	2985	†1879	3834
	15.970		29,017

*Eight months only.
†Tramp law went into effect.

The increase of population in Connecticut, from 1860 to 1880, was on an average 1.76 per cent. each year. This would give an increase in seven years of 12.32 per cent., while the increase in jail commitments in the seven years after the repeal of the law, was nearly 82 per cent., more than six and one-half times as great.

The commitments for drunkenness and common drunkards, during these same years, were as follows:

SEVEN YEARS UNDER PROHIBITORY LAW.		SEVEN YEARS UNDER LICENSE AND LOCAL OPTION.	
1866	537	1873	2125
1867	484	1874	2044
1868	575	1875	2175
1869	842	*1876	1347
1870	1050	1877	1734
1871	1290	1878	2141
1872	1470	†1879	1628
	6248		13,194

*Eight months only.
†Tramp law went into effect.

These figures show an increase of more than 100 per cent., in the commitments to jail for drunkenness, after the repeal of the prohibitory law, and in spite of the fact that many towns took advantage of the local option law to refuse license to saloons. It should be borne in mind also that the seven years of prohibitory law here given were, in most respects, the worst years for the law, ensuing immediately after the return to civil life of the Federal soldiers, with the drink-habits formed amid the hardships of camp-life, and being years during which an incessant agitation for the repeal of the law was kept up.

The general conclusions which it is safe to draw from the facts developed in regard to these four States—Michigan, Rhode Island, Connecticut, and Massachusetts—are about as follows :

1. That in these four States, during the greater part of the period in which prohibitory law prevailed, there was no vigorous and general enforcment of the law.

2. That this period was, for the most part, identical with that immediately preceding and during the war.

3. That in those years in which the law was enforced with vigor, there was an immediate and marked decrease of crime.

Proceeding, then, to consider the results in the five States which now have prohibitory laws, namely, Maine, Vermont, Kansas, Iowa, and Rhode Island, we find that the two first named have had almost continuous Prohibition for more than a generation. The other three States adopted the policy in the order in which they are named.

2, The Results in Maine.

This was the pioneer State in the movement, and gave to State Prohibition the first trial it had ever had. The initial movement leading to the adoption of the policy took place prior to 1840, and had its origin in the mind and heart of General James Appleton, a citizen of Portland, who was in 1837 a member of the State Legislature. The policy was first adopted by the Legislature in 1846, but certain essential clauses were lacking to the law until 1851, when General Neal Dow framed a bill which was enacted into law and has become known to the world as "The Maine Law." The important feature added by General Dow was the search and seizure clause.

The law became at once a political issue of magnitude. Five years later its enemies, by a political coalition, succeeded in electing a hostile Legislature, by which the law was repealed, and a stringent license law substituted.

The triumph over the law was a short-lived one. Out of the changing political conditions of that time was born, in 1854, the Republican party, which in Maine, the State of its birth, planted itself on the two issues of Abolition and Prohibition. Succeeding to power in the Legislature the following year, instead of at once re-enacting the law, it was submitted to popular vote and by a majority of 22,952 (28,864 for, 5912 against) Prohibition was adopted. The law therefore was re-enacted in 1858, after two years of license, and with various additions has remained the law of the State ever since. It was not, however, embodied in the State Constitution until 1884. Being voted on in September of that year, after thirty years' trial, it received a majority of nearly three to one in its favor (70,783 for, 23,811 against).

Twice, then, the verdict of the citizens of Maine has been taken by popular vote, once after five years of trial, and once after thirty years of trial. Twice the verdict rendered has been in its favor, and by a majority twice as large in the second instance as in the first.

In making their inquiry in 1874, the Canadian Commission already referred to, bestowed a large share of their attention on Maine. Inquiries were directed to those whose official positions gave them the best opportunities for knowing the facts, and were directed to those opposing as well as to those favoring the principle of Prohibition. As an indication of the extent to which the Commission conducted its investigation, the names are here given of those from whom they obtained responses, either orally or by letter, namely: Governor Dingley, ex-Attorney-General Drummond, Judge Clifford, of the United States Supreme Court; an ex-Mayor of Portland; Alderman Carleton, of Portland; Mr. Hobbs, of "The

Portland Argus;" Deputy Marshal Brydges, of Portland; Inspector-General Alger, of Bangor; Judge Goodman, of the Bangor Police Court; Recorder Lyons, of the same Court; Mayor Blake and Alderman Crosby, of Bangor; Warden Rice, of the State Prison; Secretary of State Stacy, Judges True, Farwell, and Bennoch, of Augusta, Rockland, and Orous, respectively; two selectmen of Orous, the Overseer of the Poor, in Bangor; the City Marshal of Rockland, and the proprietor of a hotel in Rockland.

In addition to the opinions obtained from the above men, official reports and messages are quoted from Governors Chamberlain, Perham, and Dingley, and from the Mayors and City Marshals of Lewiston, Bangor, Rockland, and Augusta.

Two of the questions asked by the Commission were as follows:

" Is the liquor law enforced, and, if not, what is the hindrance to its working? "

" What have been the results of a change from Prohibition to license, or *vice versa?* "

In the replies received to these two questions, one thing is especially noticeable, namely, that *while many, especially those resident in Portland and Bangor, admit that there is a lax enforcement of the law, yet all, without exception, testify to the good results of the law even when it is poorly enforced.*

A few extracts will indicate the nature of the replies on this point. United States Justice Farwell said: "The law being on the statute book, "even if not enforced, has a good moral influence, "as it familiarizes the people with the fact that "rum is outside of law." "Where the law is only partially enforced," said Warden Rice, of the State Prison, "it has a good influence because it "outlaws the traffic." Mayor Blake, of Bangor, though expressing his preference for a license law for cities, stated that, "although the law had been "only partially enforced, yet the sale of liquor "had been driven into the lowest quarters and "into the hands of the most disreputable class, "and that certainly the absence of the open sale "diminished drinking and consequently crime."

In fact, however great the diversity of opinion expressed in regard to the extent to which the law was enforced, there was absolute unanimity on this point, that, whether well enforced or not, the law accomplished certain excellent results. This is a point that requires explanation. Just how a law, not enforced, can accomplish such results, is at first thought an enigma. Consideration will be given to this point farther on; at present the aim is simply to ascertain facts.

An opinion of especial value, both by reason of the high position of the one expressing it and the care with which, evidently, it was given, was that from Judge Woodbury Davis, for ten years a member of the Supreme Court of Maine. On the point to which attention has been called already, Judge Davis says:

"Such laws are not valueless even in communities where they are but rarely enforced. As teachers of public conscience, the standard of which is seldom higher than human law, their value is above all price."

Speaking of the extent to which the law was enforced, Judge Davis says:

"Of our four hundred cities and towns, making the estimates below what I believe the facts would justify, I am satisfied that in more than one hundred the law prevents any sale of liquor whatever for a beverage. In at least two hundred of them it is sold only in the way that Dr. Bacon calls 'on the sly,' just as in the same towns there are persons guilty of lewdness and other crimes. In most of the other hundred towns liquors are sold probably without much restraint."

So much for *opinions* on the law and its results, as obtained by the Canadian Commissioners. The *figures* obtained were equally instructive, though the Commission was hampered somewhat in this respect by the fact that a number of the cities in Maine, especially Portland, Bangor and Augusta, " had suffered from fires that had, to a very great " extent, destroyed their public records."

The Warden of the State Prison supplies figures showing the number of committals to the prison for the two years (1855-56) just before the prohibitory law was repealed, the two years (1857-58) during which the prohibitory law was replaced with a stringent license law, and the two years (1859-60) after the re-enactment of Prohibition. A better test could hardly be imagined. The following are the figures:

COMMITMENTS TO STATE PRISON OF MAINE.

TWO YEARS OF PROHIBITION.	TWO YEARS OF LICENSE.	TWO YEARS OF PROHIBITION.
1855.......... 29	1857.......... 52	1859.......... 48
1856.......... 36	1858.......... 69	1860.......... 41
65	121	89

Here, it will be noticed, there appeared an *immediate* increase in commitments as soon as the prohibitory law was repealed, and an immediate decrease as soon as the law was re-enacted.

The City Marshal of Bangor, in his report the year after the law was repealed, calls attention to the increase of crime, as follows:

"In my report relating to matters connected with the Police Department of the city, at the close of the municipal year 1851-52, I stated that the city had been freer from crime and disturbance than during the year previous, or any year since I had been connected with the affairs of the city. This I attributed to the stringent law passed in 1851 for the suppression of drinking houses and tippling shops. This year [under license] I have to report that never, since I have had any acquaintance with the Police

Department of this city, have there been so many commitments for offences as during the year now closed."

According to the report of the same official, the arrests in Bangor for drunkenness, disorderly conduct and assaults, numbered 93 in the last eight months (1850-51) preceding Prohibition, and 45 for the first eight months under Prohibition.

Bangor and Portland were at this time the only two cities in Maine with a population of more than 10,000. In Portland, the effects of the law were still more marked. In Cumberland county (including Portland) according to figures quoted by the Commission from a work on "The Maine Liquor Law: Its Origin, History, and Results," by H. S. Chubbs, Secretary of the Maine Law Statistical Society, the results were as follows:

	For Nine Months Preceding Prohibition	For Nine Months Under Prohibition	Decrease Under Prohibition
Number of commitments to County Jails, excluding of those for violating the liquor law	279	63	216
Commitments to Watch House	431	180	251
Commitments to Alms House	252	146	106
Commitments for drunkenness to the House of Correction	*34	†8	26
Total	996	397	599

*Five months.
†For seven months.

From these figures it appears that in Cumberland county, containing the largest city in the

State, the committals were reduced sixty per cent., in the first nine months of Prohibition. In these two cities therefore, Portland and Bangor, the law seems at the beginning, without any doubt, to have been attended with a most marked reduction in crime. That this result was general throughout the State seems to be shown by the figures given by the Warden of the State Prison, and might have been inferred from the fact that in these two cities the enforcement of the law has always been attended with greatest difficulty.

The condition in Maine during the last few years, under the prohibitory law, has been the subject of much discussion and contradictory testimony. On the one hand it has been asserted by credible investigators that the law fails of its purpose, in that saloons are prevalent and drunkenness is rife. Other equally credible witnesses assert just as emphatically that the law, if it has not made an end to the traffic, has checked it to a great extent and disrobed it of its attractiveness. The only official statistics bearing directly on the question are those of the Internal Revenue Department. A special tax of $25.00 is imposed by the Federal Government on every retail liquor-dealer in the nation. As the penalties for selling at retail before having paid this tax are very severe, there are few who undertake, even in prohibitory States, to evade the payment of this tax. The records of the Internal Revenue Department show, therefore, from year to year, the number of those selling at retail in each State. But the records show more than this, especially for prohibitory States, for the payment of this tax does not give any one the right to sell liquor in violation either of State or local laws. John Smith, for instance, may undertake the sale of liquor in Maine. The first step he takes is likely to be the payment of this twenty-five dollar tax, inasmuch as his failure to do so will be a penitentiary offence, and since until January, 1888, the payment of this tax was not held to be *prima facie* evidence against him.* If after the payment of this tax, the officers of the State discover that John Smith is selling liquor contrary to the law of the State, and place him in the jail and his stock of liquors in the sewer, the payment of the federal tax does not save him. But, just the same, though he may have been selling only a week, the Internal Revenue Report includes him of course in the list of special tax payers for Maine. Neal Dow is authority for the statement that at one time, a few years ago, there were in the Portland jail forty of these special taxpayers.

So that the reports show not only the number of actual open and secret dealers in liquor, including town agents and druggists, but the number of *would-be* dealers as well. The aggregate number of all these has been for the last few years, according to the Internal Revenue Reports, as follows:

---

*The decision made by Judge Whitehouse, that the *prima facie* act was unconstitutional, was not reversed by the State Supreme Court until January, 1888.

1883 { Retail dealers in distilled liquor 1054
       Retail   "   "   malt   " 108
           Total 1162

1884 { Retail dealers in distilled liquor 974
       Retail   "   "   malt   " 103
           Total 1077

1885 { Retail dealers in distilled liquor 1014
       Retail   "   "   malt   " 80
           Total 1094

1886 { Retail dealers in distilled liquor 951
       Retail   "   "   malt   " 73
           Total 1024

1887 { Retail dealers in distilled liquor 919
       Retail   "   "   malt   " 92
           Total 1011

During these and the preceding years the State of Maine constituted an Internal Revenue district by itself. In 1888 it was combined with Vermont and New Hampshire, and the figures for the three States are given together, the number of retail dealers being in that year 2427 for the three States, a decrease of 461 from the preceding year.

Comparing Maine with the four New England States, Massachusetts, Connecticut, Rhode Island, and New Hampshire (the *manufacture* of liquor is allowed by law in the last State and the sale follows with little hindrance), and we find, by the figures of the Internal Revenue Department, the following results:

In Maine one retail dealer, on an average, from 1883 to 1888, to 610 of population.
In New Hampshire, one to .... 263 of population
In Rhode Island,   "   " .... 217 "   "
In Connecticut,   "   " .... 213 "   "
In Massachusetts,   "   " .... 242 "   "

One other thing the Internal Revenue Reports

tell us, and that is the amount of liquor *manufactured* in each State. The records for Maine during the last five years are as follows:

1883	Distilled liquor	None
	Malt liquor	"
1884	Distilled liquor	None
	Malt liquor	"
1885	Distilled liquor	None
	Malt liquor	"
1886	Distilled liquor	None
	Malt liquor	2170 galls
1887	Distilled liquor	None
	Malt liquor	"

So much for the story as told by the Reports of the Internal Revenue Department. It is, in brief, that there is practically no liquor produced in Maine, and that the number of retail dealers, including town agents, druggists, and open and secret violators of law, is but little more than one-third as large, in proportion to population, as in the four other New England States.

So far as personal testimony goes, it is exceedingly contradictory; but this has been, broadly speaking, the case, that those who were opponents of the law have testified against it, and those who were friends of the law have testified in its favor. Justin McCarthy, in 1874, after personal investigation, concluded that the law was a failure. Canon Farrar, in 1885, after a personal investigation also, concluded that it was an undoubted success. But Justin McCarthy, as well as Canon Farrar, agreed that the voice of the people in Maine was strongly in favor of the law. This appears also from the vote on the prohibitory amendment taken, as nas been stated, in 1884, after thirty-one years of trial of the law, the vote standing three in favor of the amendment to every one against. This seems to bear out the statement made by Congressman (now Senator) Frye, of Maine, in a letter to the Chicago *Advance* March 19, 1874, in which he said: "When the law was enacted I have no doubt "two-thirds of the people were at heart opposed "to it; now they could not to be induced to repeal "it."

Every Governor of Maine, from 1867 down to the present time, has publicly borne testimony to the good results of the law, the following catchwords sufficing to show the nature of their testimony in each case: Gov. Chamberlain: "as well executed generally in the State as other criminal laws are;" Governor Perham referring to liquor trade: "probably not one tenth as large" [as before Prohibition]; Governor Dingley: "has effectually closed both open and secret dram-shops in three-fourths of Maine;" Governor Robie: "has worked immense advantages for the State of "Maine;" Governor Bodwell: "nowhere that I "have been are the people so free from all the "evils incident to the liquor traffic as in this "State."

Testimonies just as strong as these *against* the law could, no doubt, be cited, but very few, if any, of them would be from public men resident in the State and daily under the operations of the law.

If one attempts to explain this uniform testimony of the public men of Maine in favor of the working of the law, by attributing it to political interest, one has still to explain why it is that political interest in Maine requires political leaders to be outspoken in favor of the law. In 1885, *The Voice*, of New York, published the opinions of Mayors and Selectmen of towns and cities in Maine. The request had been sent to the Mayor of every city having a population of one thousand or more. Of the replies received, forty-two declared the law to be an unqualified success, and the saloon to be, in those cities, entirely extirpated. In ten cities, the *open* saloon was said to be unknown, but liquor was sold in secret. In eight cities, the law was declared to be an unqualified failure, and saloons to be running openly.

Nevertheless, it is admitted that in all the larger cities of Maine, liquor is still sold, and in some of them the liquor traffic openly defies the law, and is carried on without concealment. This has been the case in Bangor and Belfast, and frequently in Portland. Neal Dow stated in 1885 that there were one hundred places in Portland where liquor was sold, not including forty drug stores. Volney B. Cushing (Prohibition candidate for Governor in 1887) said in that year that in his home—Bangor—there were one hundred saloons openly defying the law and 813 out of 1094 arrests the year before were for drunkenness. To assert that the liquor traffic has been eradicated in Maine, would be flying in the face of numberless testimonies from unimpeachable witnesses. But to deny that the law has been attended with a marked decrease of crime and drunkenness, and that it has very greatly checked the sale of liquor and the habit of drinking, is to contradict the report of the Canadian Commission, the official figures of the Internal Revenue Department, and the overwhelming verdict of the people of Maine after a trial of the law for more than a generation.

3. The Results in Vermont.

Much less interest has seemed to attach to Vermont than to other prohibitory States, partly because it is a small State having but one-half the population of Maine, and partly because of its proximity to the latter State in which the law was first tried and from which it has received the name by which it is popularly known. In some respects —chiefly the size and the inland situation of the State—the trial of Prohibition in Vermont has taken place under more advantageous conditions than in any other State. But the law itself has been by no means as stringent as in Maine, nor as in Kansas and Iowa. The teeth of a criminal law are in its penalties, and these are very light in the Vermont law. The fine for a first offence in selling contrary to the law is but ten dollars; for a second offence, but twenty dollars; for a third offence, twenty dollars and imprisonment not less than three months. The same fines are imposed for keeping intoxicating liquor for sale, and a fine of $100 is imposed on conviction of being a common seller.

The Internal Revenue Reports give the following figures for Vermont:

1883	Retail dealers in distilled liquors	454
	Retail dealers in malt liquors	62
Total		616
1884	Retail dealers in distilled liquors	439
	Retail dealers in malt liquors	47
Total		486
1885	Retail dealers in distilled liquors	426
	Retail dealers in malt liquors	59
Total		485
1886	Retail dealers in distilled liquors	516
	Retail dealers in malt liquors	49
Total		565
1887	Retail dealers in distilled liquors	448
	Retail dealers in malt liquors	50
Total		498

The average number during these five years has been 510, a proportion of one to 659 of population, a smaller proportion even than in Maine. The following are the figures for the production of liquor in Vermont:

1883	Distilled liquors	none
	Malt liquors	none
1884	Distilled liquors	none
	Malt liquors	none
1885	Distilled liquors	none
	Malt liquors	none
1886	Distilled liquors	597 galls.
	Malt liquors	none
1887	Distilled liquors	863 galls.
	Malt liquors	none

In Maine and Vermont, therefore, the sum total of liquor produced in the five years from 1883 to 1887 inclusive was 2,630 gallons of distilled liquor, most of which in all probability was for use in the arts.

4. The Results in Kansas.

The prohibitory amendment to the Constitution of Kansas was adopted in 1880, and enforcing legislation went into effect in 1881. For a period of four years the liquor dealers maintained an open fight in many of the larger cities, plying their trade with but little effort at concealment. In 1885 an amendatory law was passed by the legislature which declared saloons, breweries, and distilleries to be common nuisances and authorizing any citizen, by an action in the nature of a suit in equity, to abate and perpetually enjoin them.

With that year the reign of Prohibition in Kansas may be said to have been firmly established. The open defiance of the saloons in the large cities was changed to secret subversion of the law, many of the liquor dealers taking advantage of the privileges accorded to druggists, to convert their saloons into pseudo drug-stores, and thus continue the outlawed business. In 1887, the passage of the Murray law did away to a great extent with that subterfuge. The Murray law made it unlawful for any but a registered pharmacist to sell liquor, and required each pharmacist to undergo examination before he could be registered.

The hopes of the liquor dealers then hung on

the decisions of the courts. Judge Brewer, of the U. S. Circuit Court of Kansas, had, in February, 1886, decided that a brewery or distillery could not be prohibited and enjoined as a nuisance by the State unless compensation was rendered the owner. The case was appealed to the U. S. Supreme Court, by which the opinion of Judge Brewer was reversed (see Appendix, note A), in December, 1887. That year the last brewery was closed, and its proprietor thrown into jail, from which place he wrote, May 21, 1887, to the U. S. Brewers' Association, then assembled in National Convention in Baltimore, saying: " * * * it does not pay to keep up the fight any longer." The same year the trade report of the liquor business in Kansas City, Mo., the chief base of supplies up to that time for the liquor dealers of Kansas, said:

"Wholesale liquor dealers say they have withdrawn their traveling men from Kansas within the last six months, and that they are making no effort whatever to do business in that State. * * * * For a time after the adoption of Prohibition in Kansas, liquor dealers in Kansas City did a large business with the drug stores, but since they have been stopped from retailing liquor the trade has dwindled to almost nothing."

From the Reports of the Internal Revenue Department, and from the U. S. Census Report of population in 1880, and the State Census in 1885, the following figures are obtained:

1880	Retail dealers in distilled liquors	1821	
	Retail dealers in malt liquors	117	
Total		1938	1 for 514 population.
1881	Retail dealers in distilled liquors	1132	
	Retail dealers in malt liquors	56	
Total		1118	1 for 918 population.
1882	Retail dealers in distilled liquors	1460	
	Retail dealers in malt liquors	52	
Total		1512	1 for 784 population.
1883	Retail dealers in distilled liquors	1898	
	Retail dealers in malt liquors	51	
Total		1949	1 for 595 population.
1884	Retail dealers in distilled liquors	1948	
	Retail dealers in malt liquors	77	
Total		2025	1 for 600 population.
1885	Retail dealers in distilled liquors	2086	
	Retail dealers in malt liquors	65	
Total		2151	1 for 590 population.
1886	Retail dealers in distilled liquors	2318	
	Retail dealers in malt liquors	83	
Total		2401	1 for 563 population.
1887	Retail dealers in distilled liquors	2098	
	Retail dealers in malt liquors	84	
Total		2182	1 for 658 population.
1888	Retail dealers in distilled liquors	1277	
	Retail dealers in malt liquors	119	
Total		1396	1 for 1087 population.

These figures show a decrease in the number of retail dealers from one for 514 of population in 1880, the year before Prohibition was enacted, to one for 1087 of population in the year 1888. Especially is this decrease apparent in the last two years, since the Murray law went into force. When it is borne in mind that the figures just given represent not only all the successful violators of law, but all the unsuccessful ones as well, the decrease becomes still more striking.

The Attorney General of Kansas in his Sixth Biennial Report (1887-88) estimates that the number of places where liquor was actually sold in 1888 is less than one half the number given in the preceding table. He says:

"By an accurate mathematical calculation, based upon official reports made to this Department, I have ascertained that there is now in Kansas, in 1888, not to exceed one place where liquor is sold to every 2220 people—the smallest percentage of any State in the Union. When we take into consideration the stringent regulations under which it is sold, we are safe in saying that there is not to exceed ten per cent. as much liquor sold in Kansas in 1888 as there was in 1880."—(*Sixth Biennial Report of the Atty. Genl. of Kansas, p.* 10.)

Official figures showing the amount of crime in Kansas are furnished in the Attorney General's Report, though not as full as could be desired. The figures are given for the following years only, namely, 1874, 1880, 1881, 1887. By these it appears that the increase in the number of commitments from 1874 to 1880 was a steady one, rising from 169 to 291. In 1881, the first year of Prohibition, the number fell at once from 291 to 184. In 1885 it had again reached the figure for 1880, and in 1887 the number was 351. Comparing these figures with the population, we have:

License 6 yrs.	1874..........................one commitment for 3,132 of population.	
	1880.......... ....one commitment for 3,423 of population.	
Prohibition 6 yrs.	1881.........................one commitment for 5,709 of population.	
	1887.........................one commitment for 4,090 of population.	

These figures do not show the amount of crime since the passage of the Murray law in 1887. Commenting on the condition of things as shown by the criminal statistics, the Attorney General says (p. 8:) "Prohibition is here to stay: it is a "fixed fact. It is indelibly stamped upon our sta- "tute book. A vote of the people would never "erase it. For the good it has done and will do, "it ought never to be erased. It is depopulating "our Penitentiary and reducing pauperism and "crime to the minimum." And again (p. 9) he adds: "The saloon has been banished from Kan- "sas soil and already the result can be appreciated. "The average age of those convicted of crime and "sent to the Penitentiary, in Kansas, has increased, "a proof conclusive that the boys of to-day in "this State are not inmates of these dens of "infamy and schools of crime. The county jails "throughout the State are comparatively empty, "and the number of convicts in the Penitentiary "is growing less." This decrease of crime it must be remembered, has occurred during a remarkable increase of population, amounting to more than fifty per cent. in the last eight years.

Of course, in weighing the words of State officials in reference to the condition of things in their own State, some allowance is naturally made for a laudable State pride which may cause them to see things in a little more roseate light than might appear to a more impartial observer. But State pride is not likely to affect official statistics. In 1887 (July 12th,) the Governor of Kansas, John A. Martin, sent to the Associated Press an elaborate statement of the results of Prohibition in Kansas, in response to certain reports about Atchison. The statement (published in full in Appendix, note E.) reviews at considerable length the effects of the law on the material prosperity of the State, summing up these results as follows:

"The most wonderful era of prosperity, of material, moral, and intellectual development, of growth in country, cities and towns, ever witnessed on the American Continent, has been illustrated in Kansas during the six years since the temperance amendment to our Constitution was adopted, and especially during the past two years, the period of its most energetic and complete enforcement."

Governor Martin's letter may gain added significance in the minds of many, from the fact that prior to the adoption of the prohibitory amendment, he was not known as an advocate of it, and was currently reported to disbelieve in the wisdom of its adoption. Whether his changed attitude is attributed to the force of facts or to the force of public opinion, it is perhaps equally significant of the hold which the policy of Prohibition has gained, after six years' trial, on the people of that State.

In the year 1886, the Chicago *News* (Independent) sent to the Probate Judge of each county in Kansas an inquiry in regard to the effects of Prohibition. Replies were received from forty-nine counties, and published in *The News* December 15, 1886. In five counties, the report was that there had been no reduction in the number of saloons; in seven, the number was reported to have been somewhat reduced; in twenty-five, the report was that every saloon had been closed. In two counties the report was, no decrease in crime; in seven, a moderate decrease; in twenty-four, a most decided decrease. In seven counties, the report was that drinking had not been diminished; in nine, that there had been somewhat of a reduction, and in twenty-two, that there had been a very decided reduction.

5. The Results in Iowa.

A prohibitory amendment to the State Constitution was submitted to the voters of Iowa June 27, 1882, and adopted by a majority of 29,759. Because of a technical oversight made by the engrossing clerk, the State Supreme Court decided that the question had not been properly submitted by the Legislature, and the adoption of the amendment was declared null and void. In 1884, however, the Legislature enacted statutory Prohibition for the entire State, which has remained in force ever since, a period of but little more than four years. The large foreign population in Iowa has rendered the enforcement of the law more difficult than in Kansas, and it was not until the Clark law was passed, in 1886, giving citizens the right to bring action against saloons as common nuisances, that the power of the law seems to have been exerted.

Examination of the Internal Revenue Reports shows the following figures for Iowa:

1883
 Retail dealers in distilled liquors.....5001
 Retail dealers in malt liquors........... 283
Total ....5284—one for 322 population.

1884
 Retail dealers in distilled liquors.....3989
 Retail dealers in malt liquors........... 216
Total..4205—one for 410 population.

1885
 Retail dealers in distilled liquors 3549
 Retail dealers in malt liquors........... 229
Total..3778—one for 461 population.

1886
 Retail dealers in distilled liquors.....3769
 Retail dealers in malt liquors........... 152
Total..3921—one for 451 population.

1887
 Retail dealers in distilled liquors.....3584
 Retail dealers in malt liquors........... 283
Total..3867—one for 461 population.

1888
 Retail dealers in distilled liquors.....2928
 Retail dealers in malt liquors........... 249
Total..3177—one for 566 population.

This indicates a reduction, in the fifth year of Prohibition, of nearly one-third, in the proportionate number of liquor dealers.

The Internal Revenue Reports show the following production of liquor in Iowa:

1884
 Distilled liquors............................ 3,501,154 gallons.
 Malt liquors................................... 7,397,748 gallons.
Total ....—10,898,902 gallons.

1885
 Distilled liquors............................ 3,993,342 gallons.
 Malt liquors................................... 5,252,808 gallons.
Total..— 9,246,150 gallons.

1886	Distilled liquors	2,396,007 gallons.
	Malt liquors	6,059,167 gallons.
Total		— 8,455,174 gallons.
1887	Distilled liquors	2,036,774 gallons.
	Malt liquors	5,832,619 gallons.
Total		— 7,869,393 gallons.
1888	Distilled liquors	706 gallons.
	Malt liquors	4,968,432 gallons.
Total		— 4,969,138 gallons.

A reduction is here shown of more than one-half in the amount of liquor produced, the distilleries having almost entirely closed operations. A large number of breweries continued to fight the law until the Supreme Court decision rendered in December, 1887. As the fiscal year ends June 30, it is probable that most of the liquor reported as produced in 1888 was produced in the five months preceding that decision.

The criminal records of the State, as reported at the office of the Secretary of State by the District and County Attorneys, show a marked decrease in the last two years, since the passage of the Clark law. The figures are as follows, the proportion of convictions to population being estimated from the United States Census of 1880, and the State Census of 1885:

1882—number convictions, 1470—one for 1140 population.
1883—number convictions, 1377—one for 1236 population.
1884—number convictions, 1592—one for 1085 population.
1885—number convictions, 1339—one for 1310 population.
1886—number convictions, 1645—one for 1075 population.
1887—number convictions, 1520—one for 1174 population.
1888—number convictions, *838—one for 2148 population.

*This is for but ten months of the year, but includes in that period the terms of court.

Governor Larrabee, in his message to the General Assembly, January 1, 1888, speaks of a marked decrease, during the preceding year, in the number of commitments to the Penitentiary, in the following words:

" The enforcement of the prohibitory law has been so efficient in reducing crime, and consequently diminishing the business of the courts, that I recommend a consolidation of districts, so as to reduce the number of judges from forty to thirty-four, as I am satisfied it can be done without much inconvenience to the service, and will be a saving financially. * * During the last year, and especially during its latter half, there has been a decided falling off in Penitentiary convicts and a very large number of county jails have been empty, some of them for the first time in years."

6. The Results in Rhode Island.

The prohibitory amendment to the Constitution of Rhode Island was adopted April 7, 1886, by a vote of 15,113 to 9,230. Enforcing legislation was enacted the following month, and a Special State Police was constituted to carry out its provisions. In Rhode Island, however, the injunction clause, which has given to prohibitory law in Kansas and Iowa the greater part of its efficiency, and without which the law proved a comparative failure, has never been enacted. A vigorous attempt was made by the friends of the law in 1888 to secure such a clause, but the Legislature refused to pass it, and the law has been of late, in consequence of this omission, openly defied in Providence and other cities.

The Internal Revenue Reports show, however, a decrease in the number of retail dealers during the first year, as follows:

1886 { Retail dealers in distilled liquor......... 1425
Retail   "   "   malt   " 62
Total, 1487—one for 204 pop.

1887 { Retail dealers in distilled liquor......... 1136
Retail   "   "   malt   " 59
Total, 1195—one for 254 pop.

The following year, 1888, Rhode Island was consolidated with Connecticut in the same Internal Revenue District, and the figures for it alone are not given.

The criminal statistics for Providence, the largest city of Rhode Island, showed a marked decrease of crime during the year following the enactment of the law, as follows:

Year ending { Total arrests for all causes
June 30, 1886   except for sale of liquor............ 6473
For drunkenness, common drunkards, and disorderly............ 2617

Year ending { Total arrests for all causes
June 30, 1887   except for sale of liquor............ 4087
For drunkenness, common drunkards, and disorderly............ 1521

Showing a decrease, in the first year of Prohibition, of thirty-seven per cent., in the crime of all kinds, and a decrease in arrests for drunkenness of forty-two per cent. This decrease has not, however, continued during the year 1888. During the twelve months ending December 31, 1888, the arrests for drunkenness and disorderly conduct numbered 4140 to 3772 for the corresponding twelve months of 1887, and 4535 for the corresponding months of 1886.

7. The Attitude of the Liquor Dealers.

Such are the results of Prohibition, in so far as they can be shown by statistics and by the testimonies of public men. A few considerations more general in their nature may perhaps assist one in coming to a fixed conclusion regarding the policy.

One of these considerations lies in the fact that those who have been known as the foremost advocates of total abstinence remain, with rare exceptions, strongly, almost violently perhaps, in favor of prohibitory law, and those whose business and political interests are identified with the liquor traffic are almost if not altogether unanimous in opposition to the policy. The special significance of this is in its bearing on the question, What have been the actual results of the policy? If Prohibition had proved a failure, then one might naturally have looked for these two parties to have reversed their attitude, and to find the liquor dealers covertly if not openly favoring the law, and the temperance leaders flinging it aside.

It is conceivable of course that even after a law has proved a failure, those who have championed it may still refuse to believe ill of it. But it is difficult to conceive that those whose interests are bound up in the liquor traffic should continue to manifest such strenuous and costly opposition to prohibitory law if it had failed of its effects. It is at least a very strong presumption in favor of the success of the law, that the hostility of the liquor dealers to it has deepened steadily, until all organizations formed by them and all trade journals published in their interests are combined in a determined assault upon the law.

This fact, itself, admits of no doubt. The two most powerful organizations of liquor dealers are, among distillers, the National Protective Association, and, among brewers, the United States Brewers' Association. The former of these was organized in 1886 expressly to check the spread of prohibitory law. This was the purpose stated in the call first issued for such an organization (October 18, 1886) and the resolutions adopted pledge the members " as unalterably opposed to "Prohibition, general or local," and declare their purpose to "endorse the license system."

Their opposition was not limited to words. Graded assessments were levied on all the members, varying from twenty-five to five hundred dollars. Many thousands of dollars have been appropriated to defeat the adoption of prohibitory laws in the last three years. The United States Brewers Association has been equally emphatic and almost equally active in its opposition to prohibitory laws. The attitude of these two representative organizations is followed closely by State and local organizations throughout the land. In fact there is no difference of opinion on this subject among the leaders or the journals published in the interests of the liquor trade. It is almost impossible to find one of these journals that does not exhibit signs of agitation over the growth of Prohibition or signs of jubilation when finding what it considers indications of a decline. "Heed the lesson of the day," is the advice given in a little hand-book recently published by the attorney of the Cincinnati Liquor and Malt Dealers' Union, who continues: "The author of this little work does "not wish to appear in your eyes as an alarmist, "but he does wish to call the attention of the "liquor trade to the strides made by Prohibition "in various States, and the support sumptuary "laws are receiving from the courts, State and "Federal. * * * Brewers, distillers, wholesale "and retail dealers—all men engaged in the "traffic—stop your jealousies and petty quarrels. "You are on the eve of a great battle." It is not, indeed, too much to say that the concentration of effort at present among the liquor dealers, in their organized relations, is to check the growth of prohibitory legislation.

Placing this fact alongside the other fact, that every total abstinence organization of any prominence in the country, with the single exception of the Father Mathew Total Abstinence Union (Roman Catholic), has declared for Prohibition, and is most strenuous in the declaration in those very States in which the law is in force. It is true that some very highly esteemed leaders of opinion, who are regarded as earnest foes of intemperance, openly antagonize the prohibitory policy; but such as these are not found in States where, as in Maine, Kansas, and Iowa, the actual operations of the law are seen and felt. In these three States especially, every temperance organization and almost every Church denomination stands by the law as one whose effects are of great value to the moral and industrial interests of the community.

8. Legal and Moral Results of Prohibition.

The reason for the tenacity with which temperance men and women cling to prohibitory law even when it is not well enforced, and the unanimity with which it is opposed by the liquor dealers, may be found in two effects which invariably attend the passage of the law. These may be termed *the effect legal*, and *the effect moral.*

The effect legal consists in this, that a prohibitory law, as soon as it goes upon the statute-books, removes from the traffic all claim to the protection of the courts. It has become at once an outlaw, and has no right to appeal to the courts to enforce the payment of debts made for purposes of the traffic. Under prohibitory law and the enactments usually accompanying it, liquor (except for certain specific purposes) is deprived of its property rights, and is at the mercy of the public or its officials. And when, as in Kansas, Iowa, and Maine, any citizen is given the right, under the injunction law, to institute proceedings for the abatement of the saloon, the brewery, or the distillery as a nuisance, the basis upon which the traffic stands becomes one of the utmost uncertainty.

Even though the law is not enforced, the business becomes so uncertain in its rights, that instead, as now, of being one of the most attractive to capital, it is likely to become one of the most repellant. The expansion of the traffic is now due almost entirely to the wholesale dealers, distillers, and brewers, who, with capital to invest, are continually establishing new saloons, taking a mortgage on the fixtures and suppplying the stock on credit. Anything that checks this flow of capital into the business, by depriving it, when so invested, of all claim on the protection of the courts, is sure to strike a heavy blow at the business. This a prohibitory law invariably does.

It is this *outlawing* that seems to be most dreaded by the liquor dealers. The leading distiller of Nebraska, in a confidential letter written January 7, 1888, in reply to questions coming, as he supposed, from a liquor dealer in New York, said among other things:

"We have had a great deal of business in the State of Iowa, both before it was Prohibition and since, and we can say positively there is very little satisfaction in doing business in that State now. Ever so often the goods are seized and it causes a great deal of delay and trouble to get them released; and there is a fear of not getting money for the goods, and all the forms we have to go through make it very annoying business. It is like running a railroad under ground. You don't know where you are going or what is ahead."—*Letter from P. E. Iler of Omaha.*

The question is often asked whether it would be possible to enforce a prohibitory law in such a city as New York or Chicago. Those who ask this, in an incredulous tone, fail to consider fully the importance to any business of its *legal standing*, and particularly if it be a business done to a great extent on a credit basis. Even with every official in connivance with the traffic, and not a hand lifted for enforcement of the law, a prohibitory enactment is still certain to have an immediate and damaging effect on the business and on the flow of capital into it.

Two instances, one in Kansas and one in Iowa, are sufficient to illustrate this. In Topeka, the capital of Kansas, the saloons continued open for four years after the enactment of the law. But almost in a single hour came the death-blow of the traffic in the determined action of Judge Martin, who charged the Grand Jury to bring in indictments not only against the liquor sellers but againt the owner of buildings in which the liquor was sold. Twenty men, so it was asserted at the time, left the city on the night train to avoid arrest, and the next morning but two saloons could be found open in the city. From that day, almost, the traffic became a thing of the past in Topeka.

In Sioux City, Iowa, the law had been openly defied, no effort at concealment even being made. The officials of the city and the entire secular press upheld this defiance of the law and opposed any effort to enforce it. The public sentiment of the city, that portion at least which found expression, was in sympathy with the violators of law, and a public request was made, signed by a large number of the representative business men, that no attempt be made to disturb the existing condition of things. Yet with such an unfavorable state of things, a mere handful of determined men and women, with Rev. George C. Haddock at their head, and with the injunction law of the State behind them, began proceedings, and, in spite of public sentiment and official opposition, soon wrought terror to the entire traffic in that city. It was as much in desperation as in hate, that the assault was made by saloon keepers on Mr. Haddock, resulting in his murder. But the proceedings still went on and resulted in closing every saloon in Sioux City.

It has been sometimes urged that the repeal of license laws, and the absence of all special legislation, would leave the saloon open to prosecution as a common nuisance. In that event, however, the nuisance in each case would have to be proven : the mere sale of liquor would not necessarily constitute a nuisance. But under prohibitory laws such as prevail in Maine, Kansas and Iowa, the sale of liquor, or its manufacture, is held by the Legislature to constitute a nuisance, and the validity of such laws has been affirmed by the Supreme Court of the Nation.

Herein lies the crowning merit of prohibitory law, in that it makes it possible, under the nuisance clause, to fight the saloons one at a time.

Under a license law the saloons of a State stand together, organized and legalized. To make any changes in the law for the purpose of restriction, it becomes necessary to contend against the moneyed and political power of the traffic in the entire State. To strike one saloon effectually, one must strike all, under present conditions. A prohibitory law, once obtained, with the injunction clause added, changes this condition of things, and makes it possible to fight one saloon at a time.

A series of events transpiring in the city of Brooklyn illustrate present conditions. An Excise League was formed in that city a few years ago, whose object was to secure the enforcement of laws already on the statute books of the State. The League was non-partisan, had large resources behind it, and public sentiment as well. It prosecuted the saloons, one at a time, for violations of the excise laws forbidding sales on Sunday and to minors. In ninety-four successive cases in the first year, the evidence of violation was complete and the license was revoked; but in each case a new license was issued at once, frequently within twenty-four hours, by the Excise Board, and not one of the ninety-four saloons was actually closed. The political power of the three thousand organized saloons of the city was undoubtedly the reason for this travesty of law.

The League soon found that in striking one saloon they were striking the three thousand saloons, and accepting the necessity, great public mass-meetings were held, and thousands of dollars were contributed, and such orators as Henry Ward Beecher, Dr. Howard Crosby, and Dr. McGlynn aroused the sentiment of the city against any increase in the number of saloons. Again a seeming triumph was secured. The next applicant for a license, in a prominent part of the city, was refused by the Excise Board. But this triumph also was short lived. Resort was had to the State Legislature, and through the political power of the thirty thousand saloons of the State, the mandamus law was secured, giving applicants for license the right to appeal to the courts when license was refused. The result was that the new saloon was soon open in Brooklyn, and has remained open ever since. The League learned then that to strike at one saloon meant to strike at the thirty thousand saloons of the State ; had they carried the contest that far, they might have found that they were compelled to fight the two hundred thousand saloons of the Nation.

The god Thor, when visiting the country of the

giants, to compete with them in feats of strength, was given the task of lifting from the floor what seemed to be nothing but a large cat. The exertion of all his strength, however, was inadequate. Afterward, when the spell was removed from his eyes, so runs the old myth, he perceived that what seemed to be a cat was a huge serpent coiled around the globe. Those who have undertaken the task of closing one saloon, or preventing the grant of a license, have frequently had a somewhat similar revelation.

The other effect referred to, the effect moral of prohibitory law, is derived from the educative power of all law. " Law and government," says Dr. Arnold, of Rugby, " are the sovereign influ-"ences in human society. * * * What they sanc-" tion will ever be generally considered innocent, " what they condemn is thereby made a crime." This, of course, is not true of the more enlightened, who form their moral standards not to accord with the laws of men but with the laws of God. But undoubtedly it is true that with a large majority, conduct which the law approves is looked upon as right, even though the corollary of this may not always be true, namely, that conduct which the law disapproves is looked upon as wrong. The law is still a school-master, educating upward or downward as the case may be.

Whether or not a license law is immoral, is a question that has led to some heated argument. To a certain extent it is a question of definitions.

The intent of a license law was, doubtless, in the first place, to check the evils of intemperance and restrict the traffic in liquor within certain limits. To that extent it was what Dr. Lyman Abbott calls it, "a stigma," but a stigma not on the traffic conducted within those limits set by the law, but that conducted outside those limits. The effect of a license is two-fold, to stigmatize the unlicensed traffic and to authorize that which is licensed. It draws certain lines outside of which the saloon is to be condemned; but within which it is to be authorized and protected by law.

The ordinary saloon, as it exists to-day, is within the license limits and receives the shelter which license gives. The license may not be in logic or law, a sanction, but it is a permission; its very wording indicates this. And the actual effects which result from it are the same as those of a sanction. What the average man perceives in a license, hanging on the wall of the saloon, is an official document giving to that business a specific permission and a pledge of protection. It says, in effect, that the business is one that requires a special fitness in the one conducting it, and that the person holding the license *has that special fitness*. It is not only an authorization of the business, but a certificate of character for the proprietor, such as the butcher, the baker, the grocer, does not possess. Call in question the right of the saloon-keeper to conduct his business, and he points to his license, for which he has paid.

The State or county has given him specific authority to do this very thing; who are you to tell him he has no right to do it?

So far from the license being a stigma, then, on the man who holds it, it is, in effect, rather a commission from the Government, constituting him, in the eyes of the masses, a sort of governmental agent—one who is in closer relations to the authorities than the ordinary tradesman. It thus confers on him, in effect, a dignity rather than an odium. To sell without a license—that is wrong: to sell with a license—that is all right, for does not the Government expressly authorize one to do this? Such is the short and quick reasoning of those on whom the burdens of intemperance come with the most crushing weight, and who have the least resources, either in mind, education, or surroundings, for resisting its influences.

A prohibitory law changes this; its moral effect, just so far as it goes, is the reverse of this. It declares the ordinary sale of liquor to be a crime, and authorizes no one to carry it on. Whoever does so, does it in defiance of law, and can no longer point to the decrees of the State as a defense for his business, and a declaration of its necessity. "If men will engage in this destructive "traffic," said Senator Frelinghuysen, "if they "will stoop to degrade their reason and reap the "wages of iniquity, let them no longer have the "law-book as a pillow, nor quiet conscience with "the opiate of a court license."

It can be readily explained now why, even in localities where a prohibitory law is very lightly enforced, its repeal is still resisted so vigorously by those known as temperance leaders, and sought so constantly by the liquor dealers. Attention was called in preceding pages to the uniform testimony given in Maine to the Canadian Commission, in regard to certain beneficial results that accompanied the law even when not enforced. These were the result of these two effects which have been spoken of as the effect legal and the effect moral of the law. It may not be enforced to-day, but it may be to-morrow or next week—who can tell? A sudden swirl of politics, a sudden accident leading to an uprising of sentiment, a determined onslaught by a few men or women, the sudden impulse of an official,—any of these or a hundred other events may lead to the enforcement of the law and to a total loss of the capital invested in the business. Investments made in it to-day may be worthless next year; it has no assurance of stability. It comes to be at the mercy of public officials, and, under the injunction law, at the mercy even of private citizens. In short, the backbone of the business is gone and its reputability is vanished.

Yet saying this, it becomes at the same time necessary to recognize certain evil results attending any unenforced law. It is certain (and this applies with at least equal force to the restrictive provisions of license laws) that a law flagrantly and continually defied, brings not only itself but other law into discredit. The "majesty of the law" suffers detriment in all points where it is flouted at any one point. Premature Prohibition, that which is obtained before there is reasonable prospect of its steady enforcement, is certain to discredit itself, and is likely, in spite of the damage, felt rather than seen, which it inflicts on the traffic, to turn many of its friends into opponents.

It becomes important, therefore, to consider the reasons for the frequent non-enforcement of the law. In general these reasons will be found to have been:

1. A lack of public sentiment; that is, a sentiment that is not only strong enough to enact the law, but peremptory enough to demand its enforcement, and so organized and united that it can compel compliance.

2. Official hostility to the law, generally arising either from personal antipathy to it, or from dread of the political power of its opponents.

3. The easy importation of liquor into a prohibitory State from bordering States which are not prohibitory.

The first two of these reasons will be considered in the discussion of the party question. The third reason brings us face to face with the subject of *National* Prohibiton.

9. The Demand for National Prohibition.

The American system of Government endeavors to carry the theory of autonomy to the farthest extent compatible with public safety. Each community takes care of the things of itself. The care of highways, the public provisions for fire, the punishment of such misdemeanors as fast driving, obstructing the side walks, letting animals run at large, and similar matters local in their bearing, are relegated to the township, the city, or the county. Affairs of wider import, such as regulations for railroads and canals, laws for corporations, penalties for crime, even laws of marriage and divorce, are with comparatively few reservations on the part of the National Government, left to each State to determine for itself. Still wider-reaching affairs, such as the coinage, laws of extradition, treaties with foreign powers, postal regulations, the banking system, and inter-State commerce, come within the province of National legislation.

Under this system, all those powers known as "police powers," are retained by the State. "State legislation," says the United States Supreme Court, "strictly and legitimately for "police purposes, does not intrench upon any "authority which has been confided, expressly or "by implication, to the National Government." (*Patterson vs. Kentucky, A. T. U. S.* 501). "That [police] power belonged to the States "when the Federal Constitution was adopted. "They did not surrender it and they all have it "now. It extends to the entire property and busi-

"ness within their local jurisdiction." (*Fertilizing Co., vs. Hyde Park, A. T. U. S.*, 659,667). This disposition of authority, by which the police power, subject to certain conditions which are imposed to prevent the impairment of contracts and the depriving a citizen of property without "due process of law," can not be altered by Congress. "The courts must obey the Constitution rather than the law-making department of Government," and only by an amendment to the Federal Constitution can a State be deprived of those police powers which were reserved to it in the institution of the National Government. Inasmuch as laws regulating, restraining, or prohibiting the manufacture and sale of liquor are for the most part adjudged by the courts to be exercises of this police power reserved to the States, it follows, of course, that Congress has no right to make such laws for a single State of the Union. Congress can, indeed, levy a tax upon either the manufacture or sale of liquor and make such regulations as may be necessary to secure the payment of the tax; but farther than that it can not go. It has no right, even by unanimous vote, to enact Prohibition for any of the States.

There are, however, three powers possessed by Congress that are of great importance in their bearing on this subject, namely:

1. The power to prohibit the manufacture and sale of liquor in the territories, in the District of

Columbia, and in all forts, arsenals and military posts under Federal control.

2. The power over the importation of liquor from abroad.

3. The power over inter-state commerce.

Under the first of these (Article iv. Section 3, U. S. Constitution) Congress has the sole right (delegating it as it sees fit to the territorial legislatures) to regulate or prohibit the traffic over an area of more than one and one-half millions of square miles, and among a population equal to the aggregate population of Maine, Vermont, New Hampshire, Rhode Island, and Colorado. Six of these territories are already, at the time of this writing, knocking for admission into the Union,* and Congress has power to prescribe conditions on which they shall become States. The non-extension of slavery into new States was the entering wedge which split the Nation into two hostile camps in 1861; the same right which Congress had to prevent the extension of slavery into new States, it has now to prevent the extension of the liquor traffic into new States, should it choose to exercise the right.

The right to regulate importations from abroad (Article i. Section 8, U. S. Constitution) is one that can be exercised by the Federal Government alone. The State, except in a proper exercise of its powers of quarantine, is not only debarred from prohibiting importations from abroad, but

---
* Four of these have been admitted since writing the above sentence.

importations from a neighboring State as well. The right of the State over importations from abroad, begins only after the first sale in unbroken packages. (*Brown vs. Maryland*, 12 *Wheat.* 447.)

The most important power possessed by Congress, however, in its relation to the subject under consideration, is the power over inter-state commerce. (*Article i. Section* 8, *U. S. Constitution.*) Recent developments, indeed, indicate that on the exercise of this power may depend, to a large extent, the ultimate success of every prohibitory law enacted by the States.

There is not in Maine, Vermont, or Kansas, a single brewery or distillery in regular operation. The *production* of liquor has been stopped almost completely in those States, except for the purposes allowed by the law. Whatever liquor is sold in violation of the law is transported from adjoining States, and the State officials have no authority to prevent this. There are in Boston wholesale liquor dealers whose entire business consists in shipments of liquor to agents in Maine. There are in Iowa transportation companies whose business consists solely in transporting liquor into that State from Missouri. The companies are known to the State officials, known to the public at large, and the nature of their business is known; but there is no authority vested in the State to prevent it. To prevent the sale of liquor once within the State is, of course, a work much more difficult than to prevent its entrance had the State the power to do this. But by the decision of the Supreme Court, March 19, 1888, the right to do this rests with the Federal Government alone.

That decision (see Appendix, note F.) merits more than a passing notice. The circumstances under which it was rendered are these. There is a clause in the Iowa law forbidding a railroad, or other line of transportation, from bringing liquor into the State unless a permit has first been given by the Auditor of the county to which the liquor is to be shipped. The Chicago and Northwestern Railway, in obedience to this law, refused to transport liquor into Iowa for a wholesale house in Illinois. Suit was brought by the latter, and, the case being carried to the Supreme Court, the decision was given that this clause of the Iowa law was unconstitutional, as it conflicted with the power vested in Congress alone to regulate interstate commerce. The court conceded the right of the State to prohibit the traffic and the manufacture of liquor within its own borders, but added: "The right to prohibit sales, so far "as conceded to the States, arises only after the "act of transportation has terminated." (*Bowman Bros. vs Chicago and Northwestern Railway.*) This act of transportation, the court very plainly intimates, does not cease until after the first sale of the imported article in unbroken packages. A case directly involving this point, however, has already been appealed to the Supreme Court.

Whatever be the decision regarding the first

sale in unbroken packages, the right to transport liquor into a prohibitory State from any point outside of that State, is one which Congress alone can destroy. In all the trials of prohibitory law so far made, this has been the chief source of weakness. It is a comparatively easy task for the State of Maine to prevent the manufacture, except in very small quantities, of liquor. The difficulty has been to prevent its sale and distribution after it has been transported from another State. It is not easy to hide a brewery or distillery, or to conceal their operations, except on a very limited scale or in the wilds of mountain districts; but when the liquor has been once introduced into a city like Portland, it is a comparatively easy thing to conceal it in quart bottles, or even in kegs and barrels, and distribute it throughout the State in spite of the vigilance of the officers. It is against this great disadvantage,—a disadvantage due not to any inherent weakness in the law, but solely to the inaction of Congress—that Maine and Vermont have had to contend continually, and against which Iowa and Kansas have now to wage an unceasing fight.

Out of this condition of things has come the demand for *National* Prohibition. The question, in view of the recent decision of the Supreme Court just referred to, can no longer be considered merely a State question, since no State can adequately protect itself in this matter without the co-operation of the Federal Government.

There are two ways in which this co-operation might be secured. The more effective way would be, unquestionably, through an amendment to a Federal Constitution, prohibiting the manufacture, importation, transportation, or sale of liquor (except for certain specified uses) in the Nation. But there are two serious objections to this as a practical policy. In the first place, to obtain such an amendment requires not only a two-thirds vote of Congress to submit it, but a vote in its favor by three-fourths of the State Legislatures. In the second place, such an amendment, in addition to the strong antagonism it would be certain to arouse on other grounds, would incur strong hostility, especially in the Southern States, as an invasion upon the powers reserved to each State. As has been pointed out, prohibitory law is an exercise of the police powers now belonging to the States. Those powers are among the most important, if not the most important, which the State has reserved to itself. A large proportion of citizens who regard already with jealous alarm what they call the tendency to centralization of power, would without doubt oppose on this ground alone the transference to Congress of powers required to enforce a prohibitory amendment to the Federal Constitution. The necessity of such a course would at least have to be plainly apparent before three-fourths of the State Legislatures could be induced to ratify such a procedure. There is, however, a method in which national co-operation can be secured in much less time, and which would be free from these objections. The powers already granted by the Constitution to Congress and the President, if used with vigor and sincerity, would no doubt go very far to remedy the defects of State Prohibition. Those powers have been already indicated. They are sufficient, if exercised, to prevent the admission of any new States in which the liquor traffic is a legalized business, to prevent the manufacture or sale of liquor in any of the Territories or Federal posts, the importation from abroad, or the transportation from State to State. The exercise of these powers need not be delayed until two-thirds of Congress and three-fourths of the State Legislatures are won to Prohibition; but only until a majority of Congress and the Chief Executive of the Nation are ready heartily to second all efforts made by the States to throw off this traffic. Nor would this course prevent the adoption of a Constitutional amendment later on, if it was found necessary and desirable to endow Congress with more ample powers.

PART III---THE PARTY.

Is a Prohibition Party Desirable?

"In union there is strength."

THE keyword in the formation of a political party is—UNION. It is a union of political interests, of political beliefs, and, above all, of political purposes, that constitutes a party. Sometimes, indeed, those whose ultimate purposes are radically different may form a temporary coalition, for the accomplishment of an immediate purpose common to both, as was seen a few years ago when the Conservatives and Home Rulers of England united to unseat the Liberals. But in such cases neither party loses its identity, and when the immediate purpose is accomplished the coalition, or fusion, ends.

But union on some great moral or governmental *principle* is not enough to constitute a basis for a party. There must be, in addition, union on *some plan of action* by which that principle is to be carried out. Otherwise a party would be but little else than a school of social philosophy.

The most frequent and natural division of parties in a popular government is into Conservatives and Progressists—those who are resisting change and those who are seeking it. But inasmuch as the nature of the change sought by the latter varies from time to time, the basis of party union changes, and with it to a greater or less extent, the constitution of both parties, their methods of action, and their leadership. In constitutional monarchies, such as England and Germany, the Conservative pàrty is, as a rule, the one that upholds the prerogatives of the throne, while its rival seeks to curtail them. This gives to parties in those countries a continuity and stability which they do not have in a Republic such as America or France, though even in constitutional monarchies the changes in parties amount sometimes to little less than a complete reorganization. In England for instance the lines of division between parties change at times in a most striking manner, when some great agitation, such as the one over the corn-laws a generation ago or the one over Home Rule in the last few years, re-divides voters along new lines of cleavage.

In America the changes in political parties have been more radical, an old party having on several occasions died outright and a new party having arisen. Yet even here the party that represents, for the most part, the conservative element—the Democratic party—while it has changed its name twice, has not, from the birth of the Republic, lost its identity of organization. It began, as the anti-Federalist party, by resisting the adoption of the Constitution, and it has been, generally speaking, a party of resistance to change ever since. Nearly every amendment to the Constitution, every increase of Federal authority, and almost every marked departure or development in National polity (such as the protective tariff, the alien and sedition laws, the national banking system, the abolition of slavery, the reconstruction measures, the policy of internal improvements by the Federal government, the resumption of specie payment) has been resisted by the same party. In all this, the party has been on the conservative side, and has been true to its first traditions of resistance to the enlargement of Federal powers.

It has been different with the parties that represented the progressive elements of the nation. They have not been mere continuations one of another, under new names, but each has been a new birth, a new organization, characterized by a new name, new leadership frequently, new purposes. The old Federalist party died twenty years before the Whig party was born, and the Whig party preserved its organization and identity (though not its name) for two presidential terms after the birth of the Republican party. The reason for these new births among parties is an obvious one. A party that has been built up around one common centre as its basis of union can not readily adopt a new and entirely different basis of union without danger of dissolution. It cannot readjust itself when the needs of progress require it. A party, as a man, grows conservative with age. As a matter of fact, the Federalist party perished because it could not or would not longer meet the demands of the progressive elements of the Nation. The Whig party died for the same reason, and there are those who are already predicting the death of the Republican party for its inability to meet the growing demands of the progressive elements of the Nation. In 1854 Horace Greeley, noting this tendency of parties to grow conservative, and their consequent indisposition to give championship to new and important reforms lest their unity should thereby be endangered, advocated in vigorous terms (See N. Y. *Tribune*, July 18, 1854) the breaking up of parties at least every twelve years, if not at the close of each presidential campaign, and their reformation along the new lines called for by the new issues.

Has the time come in the progress of the nation, for a new party, and if so, is Prohibition the issue that is to determine the new party's character and dominant purpose? The answer will depend largely upon another question, namely: Whether Prohibition itself demands a new party?

One thing may be assumed at the outset of the investigation, and that is that somewhere and somehow the foes of the saloon must effect a union. It must be not merely a union on general purposes, but a *union of action* as well. All good citizens desire to see intemperance lessened, but until this union of desire develops into union of action, it can accomplish nothing in the way of political results.

This union must, moreover, be a union *at the ballot-box.* On this point there will be dissent. The advent of this question into politics has been deplored by many as an unwise policy. Moral suasion, it is urged, is the proper method for a moral reform such as temperance, and this is undoubtedly true so far as the drinker is concerned. His appetite can not be changed by statute law, nor his will-power strengthened. Moral suasion, through the home, the Church, the school, and organized societies, may be the preferable way to deal with the man who drinks; but not so with *the saloon.* To reach the saloon, to deal with the traffic, the law that is behind it must be reached and the attitude of Government must be changed. But to do this, to change the law in the face of organized political opposition to any such change, requires that there shall be a demand made at the ballot-box.

For let one stand on a platform or in a pulpit and make his demand for prohibitory law in words however eloquent, and Government pays no heed to the demand and makes no record of the opinion expressed. Let the same demand be made through the papers, in conversation, any and everywhere, for three hundred and sixty-four days in the year, and the same result follows. It is not that Government is oblivious to the desires of those thus speaking, that no official note is made of opinions so expressed; but because there is but one method by which each individual is to register his opinions and desires in regard to matters of public policy. That method is the ballot-box, and every opinion registered there by the private citizen is placed on the records of the State, and none other.

It is true that in ordinary elections the ballot is cast for men, not directly for measures; but it is generally understood, of course, that each candidate is for the most part voted for as the representative of a certain policy which is embodied in the platform on which he stands or in the purposes of those nominating him. Let a citizen express his opinion in favor of Prohibition every day in the year, and then vote a ballot that represents either silence on this question or opposition to it, and the only record made by Government is the record of this silence or opposition.

How then shall there be union at the ballot-box of the foes of the saloon? Three plans for such union have been proposed in addition to the new party plan. They are as follows:

1. By massing in one of the old parties, and moulding its policy.

2. By forming a balance-of-power party, which, while making no nominations of its own, shall vote for those candidates on old-party tickets who are best disposed to this reform.

3. By union in non-partisan organizations for the adoption of Prohibition in a non-partisan election.

1 Can the Reform be Accomplished Through Either Old Party?

The first of these methods is, as a rule, the one first to be adopted by the advocates of a new issue. Whether or not the method succeeds, depends entirely on the nature of the issue, and its relation to the basis of union on which the party has been organized and developed.

To illustrate: The Republican party was formed by a union of the elements opposed to the extension of the slave-power. This was its basis of union. To it came Abraham Lincoln, a protectionist, its second candidate for President, and Hannibal Hamlin, a free-trader, its second candidate for Vice-President. Men of widely different views were brought into union on this one dominant issue, or the one growing immediately out of it—namely, the preservation of the Union. Thus formed, the party has been able to meet and cope successfully with all the issues growing out of that first dominant issue that gave it birth. It prosecuted the civil war to a successful close. It took up, one by one, the reconstruction measures without endangering the unity of its organization. It enfranchised the negroes, redeemed the paper currency issued for war purposes, paid the war debts, including huge pension bills, still following the logical course of development from its first position. None of these issues had in it any danger to the party's original basis of union.

But it has reached, of late years, a point where

the new issues presenting themselves are entirely independent of the war and its developments, and it begins to encounter at once the dangers of division in its ranks in meeting such issues. In consequence, it has been forced to continue to appeal to its members in behalf of issues long since past and gone. Distrust for the leaders of the South has been kept alive assiduously. Pension bills have been augmented to greater and greater magnitude in each session of Congress. The treatment of the negro, in his exercise of the franchise in the South, has been carefully held up before the members of the party and made the basis for passionate appeals to their minds and hearts. But not one issue of National magnitude that has grown out of circumstances apart from the war and its results, has the party been able to meet with anything like a united front and a single purpose. Civil Service Reform has been given a half-hearted reception by many of the leaders of the party and has met with open opposition on the part of others. The growth of monopolies and the increase of industrial problems, it has been unable to deal with as a party. The reforms which the tariff confessedly needs, it is unable to make without incurring the imminent risks of party division. And to the increasing demands for legislation that shall check the evils of the saloon system, the party has found itself helpless to respond. It is a mistake to suppose that this inability is merely the result of cowardice or lack of moral sentiment in the party. Neither statement would be true; but it is a necessary consequence following from the law of the party's formation, in accordance with which men of all kinds of views and all kinds of interests regarding these new issues, were united on the one issue dominant a generation ago.

The issue of Prohibition is not one related in any way to the issues that formed the Republican party. The Prohibitionist and the anti-Prohibitionist, the total abstainer and the drinker, the clergyman and the bar-keeper, were, in the days of the party's formation, invited and welcomed to its fellowship. One was as true a member of the party as the other, provided only that he were as true to the dominant issue.

But there is a still more formidable difficulty in the way of success in thus appealing for a union of the foes of the saloon in either of the two old parties, and that is in human nature itself, and the laws that govern it in political life. The foes of the saloon have been divided between both old parties. In which of the two can they be induced to unite?

The analogies of the past give us light here. When the question of slavery was forced to the front in politics, it was done despite the efforts of the leaders in both the parties of that day, because neither party was prepared to meet the issue. That issue found in both parties the friends as well as the foes of slavery. It became necessary to bring the foes of slavery, somewhere and somehow, into unity of action. Salmon P. Chase was a Democrat; Charles Sumner was a Whig; but both were enemies of the institution of slavery. The political union of such as they and their followers, was one of the first steps necessary to the success of their desires. Had Mr. Chase insisted that Mr. Sumner and his followers should unite with himself and his followers inside the Democratic party, or had Mr. Sumner insisted that the place of union should be within the Whig party, the probabilities are that they or their followers, had they lived so long, might have been contending over the matter unto this day.

Union was brought about in no such way. Neither demanded that, while giving up nothing himself, the other give up all his political associations and turn his back on all his other political beliefs. Instead, each said to the other, in effect: Give up your old party, and I will give up mine. Step down from your old political platform and I will step down from mine. Meet me half-way in a new political organization, formed on this one issue as the dominant and dividing issue, and I will meet you. The result is a matter of history.

A condition very analogous to this is seen today. The question of Prohibition has been forced to the front despite the efforts of leaders in both old parties to prevent it, because it finds neither of those parties ready to meet it without danger of internal division. It finds the friends as well as the foes of the saloon in both old parties, and the friends are sufficiently numerous in each to keep the party in a state of inactivity. Somewhere and somehow a union of the foes of the saloon must be effected, and it must be a union not merely in purpose but in action.

Senator Colquitt and Senator Reagan for instance are avowed advocates of Prohibition. Senator Frye and Senator Blair are equally avowed advocates of Prohibition. But the former two are Democrats, and the latter two Republicans. If they effect a union of their energies and influence in either of the two old parties, two must give up all their political associations and many political beliefs, while the others give up nothing and gain everything.

In the prohibitory amendment campaigns of 1887, two being in Southern States—Texas and Tennessee—and two in Northern States—Michigan and Oregon—there were cast 415,383 votes in the aggregate for Prohibition. Of these, 246,774 were cast in the two Southern States and 198,609 were cast in the two Northern States. A very large proportion of those in the South were cast by Democrats, a large proportion of those in the North by Republicans. Any contemplated union of these voters in either of these two old parties must mean therefore on the one side the sacrifice of nothing, on the other side the repudiation of political views and associations of a lifetime. For either side to make such a demand of the other is to give the latter a good reason to question their sincerity of purpose or their sense of justice.

The claim is made at times by Republicans in the North and by Democrats in the South that a large majority of their party is so strongly in favor of restrictive legislation for the liquor traffic, that whatever laws are found to be needful may be secured in due course of time through their party. This conclusion, however, by no means follows. While it is probably true that in each party, in one of the two sections, the sentiment of the majority is favorable to strong restrictive legislation, it is equally true that in each of these parties there is a large and active minority unfavorable to such legislation, and who would resent any serious attempt in this direction by immediate withdrawal from the party. It is sufficient, in order to appreciate the force of this, to remember the large German vote in the Republican party, and the large Irish vote in the Democratic party, most of whom would not, at present, tolerate any action by their party in the direction of prohibitory law*. This minority is large enough to defeat, by a bolt, either party in all the close States, such as New York, Indiana, Connecticut, New Jersey, Massachusetts, Illinois, and Ohio; and defeat in these close States means of course defeat for either party in a National contest.

---

* By the Census of 1880 the foreign-born males of voting age numbered over three millions, about one-third being German and one-third Irish.

It would be impossible, therefore, for either party to take a stand for Prohibition without incurring at least temporary and in all probability continued defeat. The only salvation for a party in that case would be to win over from its rival recruits equal to the number of its desertions. Now it so happens that the temperance sentiment that is in the Republican party is, to far the greatest extent, in the North, and that in the Democratic party is in the South. The Republican party, therefore, in the event of its alienating a million or two of its members by an anti-saloon attitude, would have to look to the South for the necessary reinforcements to preserve it from continued disaster at the polls, while the Democratic party would be forced to look to the North almost entirely for its reinforcements under similar circumstances. To state the case is sufficient to indicate its difficulties. No student of recent American history but knows the strength of the memories and the prejudices that would prevent either party from making its losses good under such conditions. The very element in the South that is most attached to the cause of Prohibition is the one most inimical to Republican ascendancy, and the element most strongly attached to the same cause in the North is at the same time the element that is, or at least has been, most strongly attached to the Republican party. A union of these two elements seems possible, *but not in either old party.*

But has the Republican party espoused the cause of Prohibition in several of the States already, and can it not, in course of time, do the same in other States without disaster? This question arises from a misapprehension. There is not one State in the Union in which either the Republican or Democratic party ever espoused the principle of Prohibition until *after* it had been adopted by the people and become the established law of the State. In Maine, the basis of union on which the Republican party was first organized included Prohibition and Abolition, but this was in 1854, three years after the adoption of Prohibition by the State. In Kansas and Iowa, even with the overwhelming majorities which that party had in those States a few years ago, it never went so far as to espouse Prohibition. The claim quite frequently made that the Republican party gave the law to those States, is without basis of fact. It did, indeed, go so far as to submit to the people, for their decision, a prohibitory amendment in each State, but never placed itself on record in favor of the Amendment. Prohibition was obtained in a non-partisan election in each State, neither party taking any definite attitude, as a party, in regard to it.

Neither the political conditions of the Nation as they are known to exist, nor the facts of history seem, then, to justify the expectations held to by many that one or the other of the old parties will be developed into a strong anti-saloon party that shall combine in its ranks the temperance sentiment of the Nation and sweep on to a grand victory.

2. The Balance of Power Plan.

The second method of union proposed for the foes of the saloon, is in an independent organization, a sort of balance-of-power party, whose members shall refuse to vote for objectionable candidates on either old-party ticket, but shall vote for the best candidate irrespective of party affiliations, and where two candidates for the same office are equally trusted on this question, voters shall divide their votes between them according to their individual preferences.

This plan, it is urged, is the one that is pursued by the liquor dealers, with the result of terrorizing both old parties. By this method they have been able largely to dictate nominations. Why can not the temperance voters, by a similar plan, accomplish equal results?

The answer is found in this: that such a plan, to succeed, requires that its work be done in secret.

There must be, in the first place, an organized body of voters who will be willing to act with substantial unity, throwing their vote to this side or that, as their leaders direct, or as, by a majority vote, they themselves decide. This body of voters will consist, of course, in order to accomplish its purpose, of both Democrats and Republicans, who will meet together, not to make their own nominations (for that would at once constitute a new and distinct party), but to decide which of two candidates for each office on the old-party tickets they will indorse. This, of course, will be determined by vote. But straightway a formidable objection arises. Those who have been Democrats, desirous of securing good nominations from their party, have attended the primaries and perhaps the nominating conventions of their party, and by their participation in these they have bound themselves, as such action is usually interpreted, to support the nominations made. The Republican members have similarly bound themselves. How then, being already bound, can they again bind themselves to the decision of a new body of men?

The only recourse is to refuse to recognize as binding their participation in the primaries of their party. But if they so refuse, and submit themselves to a new body, and openly refuse to support important nominations made by their own party, at once the doors of future primaries are closed against them, and the bars are up to all political preferment at the hands of their party. The consequence is that all who join such an independent body of voters, at once, by that act, sever their old-party ties and render themselves unable to participate in the nominations of either old party, while, by the terms on which the new organization was formed, they are yet unable to make nominations of their own.

With the liquor dealers, it is altogether different. They do, indeed, attend party primaries, but if the character of the nominations made arouses their resentment, they do not often meet together and formally decide to vote for the other party's candidate. Instead, being a vote that has its "bosses" and follows their instructions, the work is done in secret, and while every one knows what was done, and how, and why, no one, at least none of the "bosses," has endangered his standing in his party. For the temperance voters, therefore, to follow the plan of the liquor dealers requires, first, a following that will obey its "bosses" implicitly, and, second, a readiness to work in secrecy.

In any such method as this, moreover, there is another great advantage on the side of the liquor dealers, and that is the advantage of *party inertia*. They are not seeking to reform the party, to change its attitude; but simply to keep it from making any change, and the force sufficient to do the latter would be altogether insufficient for the former. The vote of the saloon is aptly represented by a boy standing in the middle of a "teeter" who determines, by throwing his weight on one side or the other, which side shall go up or down. There is but one thing to be done, in order to deprive the vote of its present power, and that is to force it from the middle of the political "teeter" and compel it to take one end, while those opposed to the saloon take the other. The issue then can be speedily determined.

There is still another serious objection that might frequently arise under any such method as the one now being considered. In the larger cities especially, the number of different ballots to be cast by each voter is sometimes as high as nine or ten, and these may contain the names of from twenty to fifty candidates. (In Brooklyn, in the last election—1888—there were eight different ballots to be voted by each voter in one-half the wards, and nine in the other half, beside a constitutional amendment ballot.) Now a voter who had determined to vote for none but candidates who were opposed to the saloons, would be left to his own personal knowledge, (unless special ballots were prepared by some organization and distributed at every polling place throughout election day) in making out his ballot. His personal knowledge, it is likely, would differ from that of another who might be animated by a similar purpose. The names that one might "scratch," the other might vote for, and *vice versa*. The result would be apparent. Instead of union among this class of voters, their disunion would be the most complete possible, and the ballots they would cast would be as varied as the colors of Joseph's coat.

The plan for a balance-of-power party, then, on this issue, seems entirely impracticable without a radical revolution in the system of American politics. It is possible only on a small scale, or in temporary emergencies, on any issue that does not command a following blindly obedient to the behests of its leaders.

3. The Non-Partisan Plan of Union.

There remains to be considered, then, the third plan of union of the foes of the saloon, that is, in non-partisan organizations which shall have reference to this one issue alone, and shall have nothing to do with the relations of members to political parties, nor attempt to dictate to them the candidates for whom they shall vote. This is the plan advocated by Bishop Merrill, Dr. Dorchester, and others, and they point to the non-partisan contests in Iowa, Kansas, Rhode Island, and elsewhere, as furnishing abundant argument in its favor.

There can be no question that this method of union is the easiest and the quickest possible. The number of voters who are willing to join in a non-partisan organization of this kind, which does not require them to give up their party affiliations, is many times greater, as shown by the votes in amendment contests, than the number willing to join a new party. The only question to be raised is, not whether such a union is feasible and desirable, but whether it is sufficient to accomplish what needs to be done.

There are but two ways in which prohibitory legislation can be enacted into law: one is by direct act of the Legislature, and the other, by an amendment to the State Constitution, followed with enforcing legislation enacted by the Legislature. For a Constitutional amendment of any kind is very rarely of such a nature as to enforce itself. It may forbid certain acts, but it does not provide any penalty for those committing them, nor place upon any certain officials the responsibility for seeing that the law is obeyed, nor make appropriations for the necessary outlay in enforcing it. Instead, it leaves all these points to be attended to by the Legislature, and to a great extent the efficiency of the amendment is due to the way in which the Legislature performs its duty.

It is in the adoption of a prohibitory amendment that the non-partisan organization comes into play. The question then is submitted to a direct vote of the people. They vote on the question, not indirectly through candidates, but directly, yes or no, on the amendment itself. There is no requirement then for any party organization, and the custom has been at all such times for members of all parties who favor the amendment, to unite irrespective of party lines.

But it is evident that such a method of union is possible only where a direct vote is taken on the question. For our Government is a *representative* form of Government. It is only in rare instances that the people legislate directly; most of their legislation is done by those whom they send to the seats of legislation for that purpose. A prohibitory amendment is voted on directly; but all subsequent enforcing legislation must be obtained through Legislators, who are elected in the usual way as the candidates of parties. In fact, the opportunity of voting on the amendment itself can be obtained only through the action of the people's representatives. The order of procedure is as follows: (1) The Legislature votes to submit the amendment to a vote of the people; (2) the voters cast their ballots for or against it; if it is carried (3) the Legislature proceeds to enact the necessary enforcing laws.

The prohibitory amendment in Maine, for instance, provides no penalties, does not specify any method of procedure in case any one is found violating the law, in fact does nothing but prohibit the manufacture and sale of liquor, and enjoins on the Legislature and the executive officers the duty of seeing that the Prohibition is carried out. The amendment itself contains just ninety-one words; the laws enacted for its enforcement contain about seven thousand words. On none of these latter have the people voted directly, or in a non-partisan way. All these have been secured through representatives of the people, elected by the usual party action.

We find, then, on analyzing this non-partisan plan, the following features:

1. While it is the most desirable plan at the time an amendment is pending, it can not be called into operation either before that period, to secure the submission of an amendment, nor after that period to secure proper enforcing legislation,

and its vigorous execution. All that it can do afterward is to petition, unless it is prepared to assume partisan activities. But it is right at this point, namely, *after* the adoption of the amendment, that the success or failure of Prohibition is to be determined. Laws are of two kinds, those which are permissive, and those which are mandatory. For the execution of a permissive law, nothing more may be needed than the bare passage of the law. It gives somebody the privilege of doing something they want to do, and as soon as the privilege is granted they proceed to exercise it. But a mandatory, a prohibitory law, which says not, You may, but, You may not, requires something more than the bare declaration.

2. Such a non-partisan union must, it is obvious, be temporary in its nature. There can be no occasion calling for its existence, as a strictly non-partisan body, until the amendment is submitted, nor any occasion for its continuance after the vote has been taken. For *temperance* societies, of course, there is equal occasion for existence both before and after; but there can be but a very small sphere of operations for them in the realm of legislation, unless they are ready to use their ballots to enforce their petitions.

But the organizations of the liquor dealers are permanent, and their sphere of operations is continually extended into the realm of politics, reaching from the ward primary to the legislative lobby.

The advantage that results to them from this fact is a very great one, not only during the amendment contest itself, but, if it has resulted unfavorably to them, afterward in preventing the enforcement of the law. The non-partisan amendment organization dies on the day the vote is taken, for it was created not to elect men but to elect a principle. But now, when the most critcal period is reached, the political organizations of the liquor dealers find the field practically clear to them, and time and again they have succeeded in virtually nullifying the law.

The law has been brought into existence, but its parent has died in giving it birth, while the Herod who seeks its life lives on. It finds an *organized* opposition ; an *unorganized* support.

3. A non-partisan union of this kind must be, from the nature of the case, limited to the extent of a single State, while the organizations of the liquor dealers are National. If in any State, notwithstanding their advantages, they fail to prevent submission, fail to prevent adoption, and fail to prevent enforcement of the law, the power which they wield over political leaders in other States, and over the fate of parties in all doubtful States, can be called into requisition. As has been said, the National Protective Association and the United States Brewers' Association have of late years actively interested themselves in all the amendment contests, and it is a significant fact that since their activity began in this direction,

not one amendment contest has been carried for Prohibition. But they have done more than this, for they have appropriated funds to prevent the enforcement of the law in Kansas and Iowa and probably elsewhere, especially in the way of carrying cases from one court to another. To what extent their political power has been exerted upon leaders of the National parties in doubtful States, to arrest the spread of Prohibition, cannot be known; but it is not necessary to go farther than the columns of the paper in Washington, edited by the attorney of the Brewers' Association, to see that the exertion in this direction has been strenuously made.

The thought may suggest itself here that the argument that has been presented proves too much, for Prohibition has already been secured in five States by the non-partisan method. This, however, is not strictly true; in fact, it involves a double error. In the first place, Prohibition has not been secured in five States, even though *prohibitory law* has been. In each of these States where the law exists, with the exception perhaps of Kansas, the instances of culpable negligence in its enforcement are many.

In the second place, the law itself has not been secured except as the result, in some part, of partisan action, and, in greater part still, of the *dread* of partisan action. In Maine, indeed, the enactment of the law was secured at first by non-partisan action, but almost at once upon its passage its weaknesses were disclosed, and a distinct Maine Law Party was organized for the express purpose of enacting and executing necessary enforcing legislation.

In Kansas also the law was secured by non-partisan influences, but much the same order of events was witnessed there. The constant power of the liquor dealers continued to make itself felt after the swell of public sentiment had subsided. In many of the cities, in consequence, notably in Topeka, no effort was made to enforce the law for several years. At least one of the influences which defeated the renomination of Governor St. John in 1884, and secured the nomination of a candidate with views unfavorable to the law, was that of the enemies of Prohibition. That very year the question was made a partisan question. The Prohibition party came into the field with 4,495 votes. Two years later their vote had increased to 8,094, and in several congressional districts they came ominously near to holding the balance of power. Alarmed by this demonstration, the Republican party inserted in its State platform of that year a strong declaration against the saloon as a place "wherein every form of vice, immoral-"ity and crime is fostered," and made a demand for such an enforcement of the law as would " render "it impossible to sell intoxicating liquor in the "State." From that time the administration of the law changed very materially for the better. The non-partisan method in Kansas, while it secured prohibitory law, failed signally to secure Prohibition.

In Iowa and Rhode Island the partisan method had to be resorted to before the question could even be obtained for submission to the vote of the people. In Iowa the Prohibition party had attained, prior to the submission of the amendment, a vote of 10,545 votes (1877); and in Rhode Island the Prohibition party nearly trebled its vote in three years (1884-85-86) just prior to the submission of the amendment. To attribute the submission of the amendment to the rapid growth of the Prohibition party vote, may strike some as a sort of *post hoc ergo propter hoc* reasoning; but precisely similar coincidences in Texas, Tennessee, Michigan, Oregon, Nebraska and Pennsylvania, justify the inference drawn, that in each case the non-partisan exercise of power has been insufficient to secure Prohibition, or even, in most cases, to secure prohibitory law, without resort to partisan methods sooner or later.

It has been confessed, indeed, by the most ardent advocates of the non-partisan methods that these methods are insufficient to accomplish all that is to be done in order to secure Prohibition, and that they must be supplemented by other methods. One proposes a balance-of-power party as a supplemental method, and another proposes partisan action through one of the old parties, both of which plans have shown themselves, upon analysis in previous pages, to be impracticable.

4. The Objections to a New Party.

How then shall the necessary union of the foes of the saloon be secured, a union in action as well as in purpose? If it is impracticable to secure such a union in a balance-of-power party, or in either of the old parties, and if non-partisan union falls far short of the requirements of the case, there seems to be but one method left, and that is union in a new party; all who recognize the importance of this issue, North and South, Republican and Democrat, white and black, leaving their old political affiliations, meeting each other half-way in a new political organization, that shall nominate its own candidates, urge on its own campaigns, and present to the voter on election day a ballot that will mean, when cast and counted and recorded, that the voter is in favor of outlawing the liquor traffic.

This has been done, and the results have been seen in the last four years as follows: (1) A remarkable increase in the public interest and discussion of this subject; (2) an equally noteworthy increase in the amount of restrictive legislation enacted by the legislatures of almost all the States in the Union; (3) a most manifest increase in the alarm of those whose interests are closely identified with the liquor traffic. It is needless to enter into details concerning these points; whoever seeks them can find them without difficulty. To say that these results are directly and solely due to the Prohibition party, is not true. *They are due, not so much to what that party has done, as to the apprehension of what it may do and may become.*

Several objections have been urged with force against the program of separate party action. It is urged that,—

1. *A distinct party plan of action drags the contest down from the high plane of principle to the low plane of partisan politics.* This is a great moral question, it is said, and should be fought out on a high moral plane. Such doubtless would be more agreeable to high-minded men, and more in accord with their habits of thought and life. Political strife has come to smack of coarseness, self-seeking, and deceit, and the thought of active participation in it further than casting a vote on the day of election, is to many an extremely repellant thought. But after all, the question is not what is agreeable, but what is necessary to effect the removal of a great public incubus. The attitude of Government must be changed, and under our system of representative Government the only way to effect such changes is by electing men who shall represent our desires. It is impossible to do so in any other way. Whatever force this objection has, therefore, is directed against our system of Government, which renders such methods necessary in order to carry out public reforms. Besides, strife with evil in the abstract is a very different thing from strife with concrete, living, ugly evil. It is not on the Mount of Transfiguration that

one comes to close grips with the devil, and for that reason it is not ours to stay there and build our tabernacles, however exalted the place may seem to be.

But, after all, is there not something in this very objection that reveals more strongly than ever the need of carrying just such a moral question as this, which is a Governmental question as well, into the midst of political strife? If politics is a "dirty pool," is it not because it has been left too long to those who delight in dirty pools? In itself, politics should be an ennobling pursuit—the outer court of the temple of statesmanship. It is not of necessity ignoble, but only so when it becomes, instead of conflict between principles, a mere strife between place-seekers and gamesters. When issues real and great come to the front from their own inherent greatness, and the factitious issues that have been forced upon the people for the sake of mere personal or party advantage drop to the rear, then politics becomes no longer a mere dirty pool, but an arena of humanity, where the best that manhood has to offer is not too great as a sacrifice. Prohibition is, indeed, a moral issue; what Governmental issue is not a moral one as well? Honesty is a moral issue, but it becomes a very important political one at times.

2. *The distinct party method divides instead of uniting those who support the principle of Prohibition.* So it does, undoubtedly, for the time being.

Its first effect is to divide into three parties the foes of the saloon who were formerly divided into but two. But this is an objection inevitable in the inauguration of any new movement. The objection would be equally valid against every new departure in politics if it were made before all were ready to make it at the same time. When Dr. Rush inaugurated the crusade against the use of spirituous liquors, he divided the forces of "temperance" for the time being. The total abstinence movement created another division for the time being. No advance step can be taken in politics, religion, business, or in any other of the spheres of action without incurring the same objection. In inaction alone is there freedom from division. The question in this case, therefore, is not whether the party method creates further division at once, but whether it creates the most feasible basis for union hereafter. It must be remembered that the foes of the saloon are already disastrously divided into two parties, and in consequence nullifying one anothers' efforts to a great extent in the sphere of politics. The new party divides them still more, but it divides them from both old parties to reunite them in a new. Every division caused by it in the old parties means a reunion in the new party.

3. *Laws against crime are not, it is urged, proper subjects for party issues.* It is true that the law against theft, robbery, and murder are not party issues, and might gain nothing by being made so.

But if it were conceivable that highway robbery, for instance, had been made a lawful business, subject to certain charges to be paid into the public treasury; and that thousands had come to make it their daily business, and millions of dollars had been invested in it, it is quite likely in such event that prohibition of highway robbery would be an issue requiring a sharp conflict between organized parties. In the case of the liquor traffic, the necessity is not, as in the case of crime, for a mere adjustment of penalties, for the purpose of carrying out an established policy; but the necessity is for a change in the policy, a reversal of the attitude of Government from that of protection to that of Prohibition. To change this attitude requires a decisive conflict between two well-defined policies, each supported by organized bodies.

4. The most deterrent of all objections to the party method is probably this: that *the processes of formation for a new party, are likely to result in weakening the better of the two existing parties, and in strengthening the worse.* A new party, it is feared, though it may come into power some time in a remote future, will, *until then,* result in giving to the friends of the saloon a fuller swing of power and ampler opportunity for entrenching themselves in office.

The answer to this objection is a twofold one: first, an appeal to faith, and, second, an appeal to facts.

The facts are as follows. During the four years from 1884 to 1888, in which the processes of formation for the new party were most active, the result, so far from being an increase in the freedom of the liquor traffic, was a very positive decrease. In no other four years of the Nation's history, probably, was so much stringent liquor legislation enacted as during the period just mentioned. At the time of the campaign of 1884, it was very freely predicted that the cause of temperance had been "set back twenty years" by the party methods adopted by Prohibitionists. Men argued in this very natural way, that the transference of power from the party more friendly to temperance legislation, and unto the party more averse to such legislation, would result in worse laws or in feebler execution of those laws already in existence. But as a matter of fact the very reverse of this took place. There became apparent a solicitude, on the part of both old parties, and even, to a marked degree, *on the part of the liquor dealers themselves*, not to offend too deeply the temperance sentiment of the country. Merely from motives of policy, therefore, if from none other, leaders of one party felt called upon to exert themselves as never before in order to prevent a further exodus from their ranks, and the leaders of the other party had a care not to check that exodus from the ranks of their rival by flagrant acts of overt friendship to the liquor dealers.

The result then has been that more concessions

have been made to temperance sentiment, by State Legislatures, in the four years following the St. John compaign, than in the ten years preceding. In seven States (Rhode Island, Michigan, Oregon, Texas, Tennessee, New Hampshire and Massachusetts) and one Territory (Dakota) prohibitory amendments have been submitted to popular vote in response to the previously unheeded petitions of the temperance workers, and in three other States (West Virginia, Pennsylvania and Nebraska) the day for such a vote has been set. Laws for scientific temperance instruction in the common schools have been passed in sixteen States and one Territory, and by Congress for the schools under Federal supervision. In the prohibitory States of Maine, Kansas, Iowa, and Vermont, enforcing laws of very great importance have been enacted. In many other States, especially Pennsylvania, Minnesota, and New Jersey, severe restrictive measures have been grafted on the license laws. The increasing evidences of alarm manifested by the liquor dealers, have been an indication pointing strongly in the same direction.

The point that is sought to be made here is not that this increase of stringent legislation is due to the Prohibition party; but that the formative processes of that party have served rather to stimulate than to check such legislation. The apprehension that they would place a strong barrier in the way of such legislation has certainly not been realized.

5. Is Public Sentiment Ready for a Prohibition Party.

If it be admitted that the cause of Prohibition requires a new party to make it an efficient success, the question still remain *whether the time for it has come.* What probabilities of success has it? Is public sentiment far enough advanced? What other issues are in the way claiming a prior settlement at the hands of existing parties?

It is said that public sentiment is not ready for such a party or such a law. However this may be, there can be no reasonable objection urged against an organized effort to make public sentiment ready. What indeed is a party but an organized attempt to bring public sentiment up to a certain point and then direct it into certain definite action? There certainly can be no fear that such a party, which must contend every foot of the way, will come into power before enough public sentiment has been created to sustain such a law. The party that appeals to popular passion or prejudice may indeed ride suddenly into power on a swell of emotional excitement it has created, and work great mischief before the reaction comes. But there is small fear that any such premature success will attend a party that antagonizes popular passion and appetite, and which must hold men, if it holds them at all, by steady and persistent conviction rather than by temporary impulses. The party must create the sentiment before it comes into power.

But the above objection generally assumes another form. It is said that the party has no chances of success; that a vote cast with it must be, for years to come, thrown away; that, in short, the whole movement in the present state of public opinion, however admirable it may be from some points of view, is a premature movement.

Whether or not this is so depends largely upon, (1) the strength of Prohibition sentiment already developed, and (2) the extent to which it can be concentrated in a new party.

The progress made by public sentiment toward the principle of Prohibition, is best seen in the votes which have been cast for it in the amendment campaigns. Since 1880, the direct vote of the people has been taken on this question in ten different States, and one Territory. The results are tabulated below:

STATE OR TERRITORY.	Vote for Prohibition.	Vote against Prohibition.
Kansas, 1880.	92,302	84,304
Iowa, 1882.	155,436	125,677
Ohio, 1883.	323,189	240,975
Maine, 1884.	70,783	23,811
Rhode Island, 1886.	15,113	9,230
Michigan, 1887.	178,636	184,281
Texas, 1887.	129,270	220,627
Tennessee, 1887	117,504	145,197
Oregon, 1887.	19,973	27,958
New Hampshire, 1888.	25,786	30,976
Dakota, 1885.	15,570	15,337
Total	1,143,562	1,108,373

The above figures are obtained from The Political Prohibitionist for 1887 and 1888. They are official figures.

Here, then, in these ten States and one Territory (now two States) of the Union, considerably more than one million votes have been recorded in favor of Prohibition itself, as an issue distinct from party entanglements. On comparing this vote with the vote cast in each of the above States in the presidential election that dated nearest the time the vote on Prohibition was taken, we find the total presidential vote to have been 2,703,512. Two-fifths, then, of the entire vote of these States was enrolled in favor of Prohibition; less than two-fifths were enrolled against it, and more than one-fifth refrained from voting. If the votes taken by counties and cities, in 1886, in the States of Arkansas, Missouri, and Massachusetts, on the question of license or no-license, be considered, about the same proportions will be seen to have held for those States also.

The same proportion throughout the country, as in these fifteen States, would show that the voting strength of Prohibition is already four-fifths of a voting majority.

This strength, too, has been acquired in spite of the generally hostile attitude of the daily press, and the more or less hostile attitude of the "machines" of both old parties, two agencies which, when combined, are generally omnipotent in the realm of politics. When it is remembered that the prohibitory sentiment among the women of the land is still more active and zealous, the near possibilities of the movement take on a vaster form.

But can this sentiment be consolidated in a new

party? To accomplish this there must be something more than a mere belief in Prohibition; there must be a belief in it as the dominant issue. Men do not draw out of an old political party, to join a new, unless they are convinced that the new party stands for an issue of more vital importance than the old. Whether this conviction can be implanted deep enough and wide enough to insure victory, is of course one of those problems that the future only can solve. Several considerations, however, are pertinent here as casting light on the question of the permanency of the party.

Almost invariably in the history of third parties, the desire for fusion has been the forerunner of the party's fate. The temptation becomes strong, when a balance of power has been gained, to secure immediate results by combining with one or other of the old parties. The temptation may come in the form of a nomination to office conceded to the new party, or the promise of certain legislation, or a share of the official patronage in the event of victory. Whatever may be the motive prompting the fusion, the result has, as a rule, been disastrous to the new party, and for a very obvious reason. Its membership has, presumably, been drawn from both old parties, and a combination with either one is naturally distasteful therefore to a large number, who look upon such action as a breach of faith. Recriminations follow, leader becomes arrayed against leader, mutual distrust is engendered, and the usual fate of a house divided against itself is the result. The epitaph that might well be written for every third party whose remains strew the highway of history is: Fusion—Confusion—Diffusion.

The Prohibition party has steadily avoided this danger. It has done so not from the lack of opportunity, nor from a mere happy chance; but from intelligent conviction. One of the popular watchwords of the party has been: "We make no deals." This course determinedly adhered to, while it has caused some bitter feeling among those outside the party, has preserved within the party an unbroken harmony and an assured confidence in its leadership.

The party has had, therefore, if not a very rapid, a very steady and solid growth. It has maintained its National organization during five successive presidential campaigns, and in the last three its vote has been in round numbers: 1880, 10,000; 1884, 150,000; 1888, 250,000. This, of course, is a long way from anything like victory; but the growth of a new party is very apt to be in something like geometrical ratio. Each advance renders easier a next advance, and renders more enthusiastic the efforts to secure it.

Briefly stated, the claims for the party's permanence and success are:

1. *The nature of its issue.* It is clearly defined, and its advocates know exactly what they want in the way of practical legislation. They are agreed not only on the end to be reached, but on the way

in which to reach it. Its proposed reform has been tested and tried for more than a generation, and the sources of its strength and weakness are known. It is not, therefore, a mere speculation or a sentiment. It is a moral, as well as a political issue, calculated to arouse that most potent of all the forces known to history, namely, moral enthusiasm. It is an industrial reform of the first value to all classes, capitalists and wage-earners alike. It is a non-sectional and non-racial issue, appealing equally to voters of all sections and all colors. And above all it is an issue of constant and increasing importance. The evil which it seeks to remedy is one that is daily forcing itself upon public attention. The rapid growth of great cities, the immense accessions to our population, as well as the laws of appetite and avarice, combine to make the issue one of greater and greater consequence. It was not born of political change; it will not die by reason of it.

2. *A public sentiment already reaching nearly four-fifths of a voting majority of the Nation, favorable to the principle and policy of Prohibition.*

3. *A steady avoidance, on the part of those controlling the policy of the new party, of those mistakes of fusion, which have wrecked so many other third parties at the outset of their career.*

6. Other Issues of the Day.

Finally, is to be considered the nature of other issues clamorous for attention, and the effect which the new party's success would have upon them.

Political corruption has become one of the most urgent of these issues.

The relation which the saloon bears to this evil, in its present form, has been pointed out in previous pages. But would not the new party, as it came into power, become equally corrupt with the old parties? Naturally, it would then attract place-seekers and spoilsmen, and the morals of the party would suffer. The approach to success would doubtless bring to this as to all other parties increased temptations and a diminution in the purity of its methods. But it would have cut itself loose, of necessity, from the saloon, and from those methods of corruption which can be made successful on a large scale only through the saloon. Moreover, a campaign on a really important issue, moral as well as political, is sure to bring to the front moral leaders and to relegate to the rear the mere wire-pullers and tricksters. It is when a party becomes devoid of any such issues that it has to depend so implicitly upon the "machine" and those skilled in manipulating it.

Tariff Reform is another issue that has been more or less prominent throughout the history of the Nation, and which, so long as there is a tariff, will continue to demand attention from time to time. But this issue, so far as it is made an issue at all between the two old parties, consists entirely in matters of detail. So far as platform utterances go, both parties stand on the same ground in respect to the tariff, since both declare in favor of a readjustment of rates, and neither declares for free trade. On the details of readjustment there is conflict; on the need of *some* sort of readjustment there is agreement. The Democratic House has one tariff reform bill and the Republican Senate has another, and the only question is which better meets the industrial needs of the Nation. To determine this requires a mastery of the details of the tariff and of industrial conditions which few voters can hope to obtain.

If there is any issue that suffers from being made a partisan question it is the issue of Tariff Reform. It is about the last question in the world that should be settled by means of popular vote, for it is one the average voter can not, from the very nature of the case, pass judgment upon with comprehensive intelligence. The lumberman of Maine may be well-fitted to decide what the effect of a certain schedule of rates on lumber would be; but how is he to come to an intelligent opinion on the precise duty that should be placed on pig iron or steel rails? Or what can the iron merchant ordinarily know regarding the exact per cent. of duty that should be placed on cut lumber? The miner of Michigan and the potter of New Jersey know the conditions each of his own industry, but what means has either of deciding whether the rate on the other's product can be safely lowered ten or twenty per cent? In fact, as a general rule, the only particulars in which the average voter is competent to decide, are the very ones in which his own self-interest is likely to bias his decision. It becomes, therefore, a conflict mainly of local and selfish interests.

If it were a question between free trade and protection, a question, that is, between principles and not details, the lumberman of Maine, the iron worker of Pennsylvania, the potter of Jersey, the miner of Michigan, the wool-grower of Ohio, and the sugar planter of Louisiana, might all be equally fitted to decide, and, what is better, those whose self-interest was not directly involved would be equally competent, or more so, to form a correct conclusion. But it is no such issue and neither party can make such an issue as at present constituted. Nor, indeed, can either party approach the question of details with anything like an harmonious spirit. Tariff Reform with both old parties, has become, under such circumstances, a mere playing for points, a strife for party advantage. The Democratic bill puts salt, a Northern product chiefly, on the free list, but leaves a duty of over sixty per cent., on sugar, a Southern product chiefly. The Republican bill retaliates by leaving the duty on salt undisturbed, but cutting down the duty on sugar fifty per cent. The Congressman of upper New York votes, as one admitted to the writer not long ago, for a high duty on hops, to keep out those of Canadian growth, but for free trade in hop-poles so that his constitutents could purchase them at the cheapest rates. The only wise plan of regulating equitably the tariff rates from year to year or from decade to decade, seems to be by a commission of industrial experts, such as was constituted by Congress a few years ago, before which all interests have a hearing, and by which a readjustment of rates according to the industrial needs of the nation, and not the needs of partisanship, may be expected.

The Labor Problems of the day are clamorous, but chaotic. Who can tell just what they are, much less just what they demand? What plan of *action* could possibly form the basis of a united labor party? What is the specific legislation on which the labor interests are agreed? In the last presidential campaign there were five distinct parties, each claiming to be a labor party, in the field, namely, Union Labor, United Labor, Greenback, Industrial Reform, and Socialists.

A free ballot and a fair count is to many voters an issue of supreme importance, but is, again, an issue which neither old party seems capable of settling, doubtless because both share in the guilt of corrupting the ballot-box where they have power enough to do so with impunity. Just how much of 'fact there is in the representations made concerning the way in which the negro in some of the Southern States is defrauded of his ballot, it is difficult to tell. But this is certain, that twenty-four years of Republican ascendancy in the White House failed to correct the evil, or indeed, if the representations of some Republican leaders are to be credited, even to check it. The same conditions seem to have prevailed under Republican as under Democratic ascendancy. Either the evil is one that can not be reached by Federal interference, or both parties have shamelessly neglected to reach it. And if it can be remedied only by State action, the fact that in the last campaign the Republican party entirely abandoned the field in many of the Southern States, making no State nominations and no campaign, seems to indicate that if the remedy is to come at all it must be by some other channel than that party.

In fact, the day of distinct issues between the two old parties has to all present appearances passed away. Their issues now are factitious ones, differing with different localities, changing from one year to another in the same locality. Their appeals are almost wholly appeals to past records or bitter assaults upon the honesty and patriotism of their opponents. It is a strife of ins and outs. Years ago Ralph Waldo Emerson said:

"From neither party, when in power, has the world any benefit to expect in science, art, or humanity, at all commensurate with the resources of the nation."—(*Emerson's "Essay on Politics."*)

And again he says:

"The vice of our leading parties in this country is that they do not plant themselves on the deep and necessary grounds to which they are respectively entitled, but lash themselves to fury in the carrying of some local and momentary measure, nowise useful to the Commonwealth."

What Emerson described as the condition of affairs a few years ago, a careful student of American politics describes as the condition to-day. In his work on "The American Commonwealth," which has won such high encomiums from all critics, Prof. Bryce, of Edinburgh, says:

"This election [1876] marks the close of the third period, which embraces the rise and overwhelming predominance of the Republican party. Formed to resist the extension of slavery, led on to destroy it, compelled by circumstances to expand the central authority in a way unthought of before, that party had now worked out its program and fulfilled its original mission. The old aims were accomplished, but new ones had not yet been substituted, for though new problems had appeared, the party was not prepared with solutions. Similarly the Democratic party had discharged its mission in defending the rights of the reconstructed States and criticising excesses of executive power; similarly it too had refused to grapple either with the fresh questions which had begun to arise since the war, or with those older questions which had now reappeared above the subsiding flood of war-days. The old parties still stood as organizations, and still claimed to be the exponents of principles. Their respective principles had, however, little direct application to the questions which confronted and divided the Nation. A new era was opening, which called either for the evolution of new parties or for the transformation of the old ones by the adoption of tenets, and the advocacy of views suited to the needs of the time. But this fourth period, which began with 1876, has not yet seen such a transformation, and we shall therefore find, when we come to examine the existing state of parties, that there is an unreality and lack of vital force in both Republicans and Democrats, powerful as their organizations are."—(*The American Commonwealth, vol. II., p.* 648.)

"The American parties now continue to exist because they have existed. The mill has been constructed and its machinery goes on turning even when there is no grist to grind."—*p.* 656.

In designating the new issues which have arisen since the war and are now calling for settlement, Professor Bryce first mentions the treatment of the liquor traffic. He says·

" That [new issue] which most keenly interests the people, though of course not all the people, is the regulation or extinction of the liquor traffic. On this neither party has committed or will commit itself. * * * * Practically for both parties the point of consequence is what they can gain or lose. Each has clearly something to lose. The drinking part of the population is chiefly foreign. Now the Irish are mainly Democrats, so the Democratic party dare not offend them. The Germans are mainly Republicans, so the Republicans are equally bound over to caution."—*p.* 657.

Such is the condition as seen by a careful observer, who has the additional advantage of observing American politics as an outsider. Two parties, marshalling their forces each year in heated conflict over nobody knows what. A tremendous expenditure of energy and money, accompanied generally with a deluge of unsavory personalities for the lack of better campaign material, and with demoralization to business, in order to decide, not a great question of national polity, but whether one set of politicians or another shall enter upon the offices. "The mill has been constructed and "its machinery goes on turning even when there "is no grist to grind."

The appeal can be made with confidence, to any candid voter, Republican or Democrat, if the conditions of political life in our country to-day do not tally very closely with those described by the historian Froude, in speaking of another Republic of earlier times. Mr. Froude said:

"The essential causes of difference had ceased, but two traditional parties still contended for supremacy, and as the distinctions grew more unreal, the more bitter faction became. Men of real ability, to whatever party they belonged, thought at heart very much alike. They knew that they could not stand still in a world of change, and they knew that if they let the horses run away there was risk of an overturn. When there was no longer any question of principle, the contention of parties in the Legislature degenerated into a struggle for power, and the chiefs on both sides were driven forward by a fatal necessity to raise new questions, to excite new hopes, and to appeal to passion to decide on problems which required the coolest reason. However able a man was, he could not do his ability justice. His duty was to his party—his party first, his country after. Statesmen might see the truth, but they dared not act upon it. They were arranged in opposite camps, each advocating one set of opinions only, and denouncing their rivals as public enemies. They had often to thwart what they knew to be good, and to advocate what they really disapproved. If the result was music, the music was made out of discord. A genuine patriot could only exclaim, 'A plague o' both your houses.' "—(*Address by James Anthony Froude, Nov.* 3, 1882, *on* "*A Lesson on Democracy,*" *before the Birmingham Institute.*)

The peril of this condition of things described by Mr. Froude, is greatly increased in this country by the fact that here this division of parties is to such a great extent a sectional division. No patriot can view with other than feelings of regret the array of the virtuous and intelligent in one section against those of the same character in another section, not because of any vital difference in belief or patriotic purpose, but by reason of the passions of a war ended nearly a quarter of a century ago, and by reason of the distrust kept alive by political leaders of both sections for partisan ends. The division, as has been said, is an unnatural one. Twenty-five years of political strife have left every Southern State in the Democratic column, and every Northern State, excepting Connecticut, in the Republican column. (Election of 1888.) Such a division is fraught with opportunities for mischief, especially when played upon by political demagogues. Questions of finance and of political economy have failed to obliterate the dividing lines left by the war. Is it not hopeless to expect that anything short of a readjustment of voters along new lines will accomplish the desired result? There is certainly no issue now in politics so likely to accomplish this new alignment of parties as Prohibition.

So far, then, from it's being too soon for the new party, the time is really over-due. The opportunity is ripe, and has been for years. A more favorable conjunction of circumstances it would be difficult to conceive. The yearly surplus in the Federal Treasury just about equals the revenue from the Federal tax on liquors. The removal of this tax, therefore, instead of requiring new methods of taxation, would relieve the Nation of a heavy incubus and a constant temptation to extravagance and corruption. No interests of the Nation would suffer from a new readjustment of voters; some of its dearest interests would derive therefrom inestimable gain.

APPENDIX.

NOTE A.

U. S. SUPREME COURT.

PETER MUGLER
v.
THE STATE OF KANSAS.
} 2 CASES.

AND

THE STATE OF KANSAS
v,
ZIEBOLD & HAGELIN.
} 1 CASE.

OCTOBER TERM, 1887.

Nos. 19 and 20. PETER MUGLER, plaintiff in error, *v.* THE STATE OF KANSAS.

In error to the Supreme Court of the State of Kansas.

No. 934. THE STATE OF KANSAS EX REL. J. F. TUFTS, Assistant Attorney-General of the State of Kansas for Atchison County, Kan., appellant, *v.* HERMAN ZIEBOLD and JOSEPH HAGELIN, partners as ZIEBOLD & HAGELIN.

Appeal from the Circuit Court of the United States for the District of Kansas.

MR. JUSTICE HARLAN delivered the opinion of the court.

These cases involve an inquiry into the validity of certain statutes of Kansas relating to the manufacture and sale of intoxicating liquors. The first two are indictments charging Mugler, the plaintiff in error, in one case, with having sold, and in the other, with having manufactured spirituous, vinous, malt, fermented and other intoxicating liquors, in Saline County, Kansas, without having the license or permit required by the statute. The defendant, having been found guilty, was fined in each case $100, and ordered to be committed to the county jail until the fine was paid. Each judgment was affirmed by the Supreme Court of Kansas, and thereby it is contended, the defendant was denied rights, privileges, and immunities guaranteed by the Constitution of the United States.

The third case—State of Kansas, *ex rel.*, etc , *v.* Ziebold, etc.—was commenced by petition filed in one of the courts of the State. The relief sought is:

1. That the group of buildings constituting the brewery of the defendants, partners, as Ziebold & Hagelin, in Atchison County, Kan., be adjudged a common nuisance, and the sheriff, or other proper officer, directed to shut up or abate the same.

2. That the defendants be enjoined from using or permitting to be used, the said premises as a place where intoxicating liquors may be sold, bartered or given away, or kept for barter· sale, or gift, otherwise than by authority of law.

The defendants answered, denying the allegations of the petition, and averring:

1. That said buildings were erected by them prior to the adoption by the people of Kansas of the Constitutional Amendment prohibiting the manufacture and sale of intoxicating liquors for other than medicinal, scientific, and mechanical purposes, and before the passage of the prohibitory liquor statute of that State.

2. That they were erected for the purpose of manufacturing beer, and cannot be put to any other use; and, if not so used, they will be of little value.

3. That the statute under which said suit was brought, is void under the Fourteenth Amendment of the Constitution of the United States.

* * * * * * * * * *

The facts necessary to a clear understanding of the questions common to these cases are the following: Mugler, and Ziebold & Hagelin were engaged in manufacturing beer at their respective establishments (constructed specially for that purpose) for several years prior to the adoption of the Constitutional Amendment of 1880. They continued in such business in defiance of the statute of 1881, and without having the required permit. Nor did Mugler have a license or permit to sell beer. The single sale of which he was found guilty occurred in the State, and after May 1st, 1881—that is, after the Act of February 19th, 1881, took effect—and was of beer manufactured before its passage.

The buildings and machinery constituting these breweries are of little value if not used for the purpose of manufacturing beer; that is to say, if the statutes are enforced against the defendants the value of their property will be very materially diminished.

The general question in each case is whether the foregoing statutes of Kansas are in conflict with that clause of the Fourteenth Amendment, which provides that,

"No State shall make or enforce any law which shall abridge the privileges or immunities of citizens of the United States, nor shall any State deprive any person of life, liberty, or property, without due process of law."

That legislation by a State prohibiting the manufacture within her limits of intoxicating liquors, to be there sold or bartered for general use as a beverage, does not necessarily infringe any right, privilege, or immunity secured by the Constitution of the United States, is made clear by the decisions of this court, rendered before and since the adoption of the Fourteenth Amendment; to some of which, in view of questions to be presently considered, it will be well to refer.

In the License Cases, 5 How. 504, the question was whether certain statutes of Massachusetts, Rhode Island, and New Hampshire, relating to the sale of spirituous liquors, were repugnant to the Constitution of the United States.

In determining that question it became necessary to inquire whether there was any conflict between the exercise by Congress of its power to regulate commerce with foreign countries, or among the several States, and the exercise by a State of what are called police powers. Although the members of the court did not fully agree as to the grounds upon which the decision should be placed, they were unanimous in holding that the statutes then under examination were not inconsistent with the Constitution of the United States, or with any act of Congress. Chief Justice Taney said:

"If any State deems the retail and internal traffic in ardent spirits injurious to its citizens, and calculated to produce idleness, vice, or debauchery, I see nothing in the Constitution of the United States to prevent it from regulating and restraining the traffic, or from prohibiting it altogether, if it thinks proper."

Mr. Justice McLean, among other things, said:

"A State regulates its domestic commerce, contracts, and transmission of estates, real and personal, and acts upon internal matters which relate to its moral and political welfare. Over these subjects the Federal Government has no power. The acknowledged police power of a State extends often to the destruction of property. A nuisance may be abated. Everything prejudicial to the health or morals of a city may be removed."

Mr. Justice Woodbury observed:

"How can they (the States) be sovereign within their respective spheres, without power to regulate all their internal commerce, as well as police, and direct how, when and where it shall be conducted in articles intimately connected either with public morals or public safety or public prosperity?"

Mr. Justice Grier, in still more emphatic language, said:

"The true question presented by these cases, and one which I am not disposed to evade, is whether the States have a right to prohibit the sale and consumption of an article of commerce which they believe to be pernicious in its effects, and the cause of disease, pauperism, and crime. Without attempting to define what are the peculiar subjects or limits of this power, it may safely be affirmed that every law for the restraint or punishment of crime, for the preservation of the public peace, health, and morals, must come within this category.

"It is not necessary, for the sake of justifying the State legislation now under consideration, to array the appalling statistics of misery, pauperism, and crime which have their origin in the use or abuse of ardent spirits. The police power, which is exclusively in the States, is alone competent to the correction of these great evils, and all measures of restraint or prohibition necessary to effect the purpose, are within the scope of that authority."

In Bartemeyer v. Iowa, 18 Wall. 129, it was said that prior to the adoption of the Fourteenth Amendment, State enactments, regulating or prohibiting the traffic in intoxicating liquors, raised no question under the Constitution of the United States; and that such legislation was left to the discretion of the respective States, subject to no other limitations than those imposed by their own Constitutions, or by the general principles supposed to limit all legislative power. Referring to the contention that the right to sell intoxcating liquors was secured by the Fourteenth Amendment, the court said that "so far as such a right exists, it is not one of the rights growing out of citizenship of the United States." In Beer Company v. Massachusetts, 97 U. S. 33, it was said that. "as a measure of police regulation, looking to the preservation of public morals, a State law prohibiting the manufacture and sale of intoxicating liquors is not repugnant to any clause of the Constitution of the United States."

Finally, in Foster v. Kansas, 112 U. S. 206, the court said that the question as to the constitutional power of a State to prohibit the manufacture and sale of intoxicating liquors was no longer an open one in this court. These cases rest upon the acknowledged right of the several States of the Union to control their purely internal affairs, and, in so doing, to protect the health, morals, and safety of their people by regulations that do not interfere with the execution of the powers of the General Government, or violate rights secured by the Constitution of the United States. The power to establish such regulations, as was said in Gibbons v. Ogden, 9 Wheat. 203, reaches everything within the territory of a State not surrendered to the National Government.

It is, however, contended that, although the State may prohibit the manufacture of intoxicating liquors for sale or barter within her limits, for general use as a beverage, "no convention or Legislature has the right, under our form of government, to prohibit any citizen from manufacturing for his own use, or for export, or storage any article of food or drink not endangering or affecting the rights of others." The argument made in support of the first branch of this proposition briefly stated, is:

That in the implied compact between the State and the citizen, certain rights are reserved by the latter which are guaranteed by the constitutional provision protecting persons against being deprived of life, liberty or property, without due process of law, and with which the State cannot interfere; that among those rights is that of manufacturing for one's own use either food or drink; and that while, according to the doctrines of the Commune, the State may control the tastes, appetites, habits, dress, food, and drink of the people, our system of government, based upon the individuality and intelligence of the citizen, does not claim to control him, except as to his conduct to others, leaving him the sole judge as to all that only affects himself.

It will be observed that the proposition, and the argument made in support of it, equally concede that the right to manufacture drink for personal use is subject to the condition that such manufacture does not endanger or affect the rights of others. If such manufacture does prejudicially affect the rights and interests of the community, it follows, from the very premises stated, that society has the power to protect itself, by legislation, against the injurious consequences of that business. As was said in Munn *v.* Illinois, 94 U. S. 124: " While power does not exist with the whole people to control rights that are purely and exclusively private, Government may require each citizen to so conduct himself, and so use his own property, as not unnecessarily to injure another."

But by whom, or by what authority, is it to be determined whether the manufacture of particular articles of drink, either for general use or for the personal use of the maker, will injuriously affect the public? Power to determine such questions, so as to bind all, must exist somewhere; else society will be at the mercy of the few, who, regarding only their own appetites or passions, may be willing to imperil the peace and security of the many, provided only they are permitted to do as they please. Under our system that power is lodged with the legislative branch of the Government. It belongs to that department to exert what are known as the police powers of the State, and to determine, primarily, what measures are appropriate or needful for the protection of the public morals, the public health, or the public safety.

It does not at all follow that every statute enacted ostensibly for the promotion of these ends, is to be accepted as a legitimate exertion of the police powers of the State. There are, of necessity, limits beyond which legislation cannot rightfully go. While every possible presumption is to be indulged in favor of the validity of a statute, Sinking Fund Cases, 99 U. S. 718, the courts must obey the Constitution rather than the law-making department of Government, and must, upon their responsibility, determine whether, in any particular case, these limits have been passed.

"To what purpose," it was said in Marbury *v.* Madison, 1 Cranch, 137, 167, "are powers limited, and to what purpose is that limitation committed to writing, if these limits may, at any time, be passed by those intended to be restrained? The distinction between a government with limited and unlimited powers is abolished, if those limits do not confine the persons on whom they are imposed, and if acts prohibited and acts allowed are of equal obligation." The courts are not bound by mere forms, nor are they to be misled by mere pretences. They are at liberty—indeed, are under a solemn duty—to look at the substance of things, whenever they enter upon the inquiry whether the Legislature has transcended the limits of its authority. If, therefore, a statute purporting to have been enacted to protect the public health, the public morals or the public safety, has no real or substantial relation to those objects, or is a palpable invasion of rights secured by the fundamental law, it is the duty of the courts to so adjudge, and thereby give effect to the Constitution.

Keeping in view these principles as governing the relations of the judicial and legislative departments of Government with each other, it is difficult to perceive any ground for the judiciary to declare that the prohibition by Kansas of the manufacture or sale within her limits of intoxicating liquors for general use there as a beverage, is not fairly adapted to the end of protecting the community against the evils which confessedly result from the excessive use of ardent spirits. There is here no justification for holding that the State, under the guise merely of police regulations, is aiming to deprive the citizen of his constitutional rights; for we cannot shut out of view the fact, within the knowledge of all, that the public health, the public morals, and the public safety, may be endangered by the general use of intoxicating drinks; nor the fact, established by statistics accessible to every one, that the disorder, pauperism, and crime prevalent in the country, are in some degree at least traceable to this evil.

If, therefore, a State deems the absolute prohibition of the manufacture and sale within her limits of intoxicating liquors for other than medical, scientific, and manufacturing purposes, to be necessary to the peace and security of society, the courts cannot, without usurping legislative functions, override the will of the people as thus expressed by their chosen representatives. They have nothing to do with the mere policy of legislation. Indeed, it is a fundamental principle in our institutions, indispensable to the preservation of public liberty, that one of the separate departments of Government shall not usurp powers committed by the Constitution to another department. And so, if, in the judgment of the Legislature, the manufacture of intoxicating liquors for the maker's own use as a beverage, would tend to cripple, if it did not defeat, the effort to guard the community against the evils attending the excessive use of such liquors, it is not for the courts, upon their views as to what is best and safest for the community, to disregard the legislative determination of that question.

* * * * * * * * * *

The power which the States unquestionably have of prohibiting such use by individuals of their property as will be prejudicial to the health, the morals, or the safety of the public, is not, and—consistently with the existence and safety of organized society—cannot be burdened with the condition that the State must compensate such individual owners for pecuniary losses they sustain, by reason of their not being permitted by a noxious use of their property, to inflict injury upon the community. The exercise of the police power by the destruction of property which is itself a public nuisance, or the prohibition of its use in a particular way, whereby its value becomes depreciated, is very different from taking property for public use, or from depriving a person of his property without due process of law. In the one case, a nuisance only is abated; in the other, unoffending property is taken away from an innocent owner.

It is true, that, when the defendants in these cases purchased or erected their breweries, the laws of the State did not forbid the manufacture of intoxicating liquors. But the State did not thereby give any assurance, or come under an obligation, that its legislation upon that subject would remain unchanged. Indeed, as was said in Stone v. Mississippi, 101 U. S., the supervision of the public health and the public morals is a Governmental power, " continuing in its nature," and " to be dealt with as the special exigencies of the moment may require;" and that, " for this purpose, the largest legislative discretion is allowed, and the discretion cannot be parted with any more than the power itself."

So in Beer Company v. Massachusetts, 97 U. S. 32:

"If the public safety or the public morals require the discontinuance of any manufacture or traffic, the hand of the Legislature cannot be stayed from providing for its discontinuance by any incidental inconvenience which individuals or corporations may suffer."

It now remains to consider certain questions relating particularly to the thirteenth section of the Act of 1885. That section is as follows:

"SECTION 13. All places where intoxicating liquors are manufactured, sold, bartered or given away in violation of any of the provisions of this act, or where intoxicating liquors are kept for sale, barter or delivery in violation of this act, are hereby declared to be common nuisances, and upon the judgment of any court having jurisdiction finding such place to be a nuisance under this section, the sheriff, his deputy, or under-sheriff, or any constable of the proper county, or marshal of any city where the same is located, shall be directed to shut up and abate such place by taking possession thereof and destroying all intoxicating liquors found therein, together with all signs, screens, bars, bottles, glasses, and other property used in keeping and maintaining said nuisance; and the owner or keeper thereof shall, upon conviction, be adjudged guilty of maintaining a common nuisance, and shall be punished by a fine of not less than $100, nor more than $500, and by imprisonment in the county jail not less than thirty days nor more than ninety days. The Attorney-General, County Attorney, or any citizen of the county where such nuisance exists, or is kept, or is maintained, may maintain an action in the name of the State to abate and perpetually enjoin the same. The injunction shall be granted at the commencement of the action, and no bond shall be required. Any person violating the terms of any injunction granted in such proceeding, shall be punished as for contempt, by a fine of not less than $100 nor more than $500, or by imprisonment in the county jail not less than thirty days nor more than six months, or by both such fine and imprisonment, in the discretion of the court."

It is contended in the case of Kansas *v.* Ziebold & Hagelin, that the entire scheme of this section is an attempt to deprive persons who come within its provisions of their property and of their liberty without due process of law; especially, when taken in connection with that clause of Section 14 (amendatory of Section 21 of the Act of 1881) which provides that "in prosecutions under this act, by indictment or otherwise . . . it shall not be necessary in the first instance for the State to prove that the party charged did not have a permit to sell intoxicating liquors for the excepted purposes."

We are unable to perceive anything in these regulations inconsistent with the constitutional guarantees of liberty and property. The State having authority to prohibit the manufacture and sale of intoxicating liquors for other than medical, scientific, and mechanical purposes, we do not doubt her power to declare that any place, kept and maintained for the illegal manufacture and sale of such liquors, shall be deemed a common nuisance, and be abated, and at the same time to provide for the indictment and trial of the offender. One is a proceeding against the property used for forbidden purposes, while the other is for the punishment of the offender.

It is said that by the thirteenth section of the Act of 1885, the Legislature, finding a brewery within the State in actual operation, without notice, trial, or hearing, by the mere exercise of its arbitrary caprice, declares it to be a common nuisance, and then prescribes the consequences which are to follow inevitably by judicial mandate required by the statute, and involving and permitting the exercise of no judicial discretion or judgment; that, the brewery being found in operation, the court is not to determine whether it is a common nuisance, but, under the command of the statute, is to find it to be one; that it is not the liquor made, or the making of it, which is thus enacted to be a common nuisance, but the place itself, including all the property used in keeping and maintaining the common nuisance; that the judge, having thus signed without inquiry, and it may be against the fact and against his own judgment, the edict of the Legislature, the court is commanded by its officers to take possession of the place and shut it up; nor is all this destruction of property, by legislative edict, to be made as a forfeiture consequent upon conviction of any offence, but merely because the Legislature so commands; and it is done by a court of equity, without any previous conviction first had, or any trial known to the law.

This, certainly, is a formidable arraignment of the legislation of Kansas, and if it were founded upon a just interpretation of her statutes, the court would have no difficulty in declaring that they could not be enforced without infringing the constitutional rights of the citizen.

But these statutes have no such scope and are not attended with any such results as the defendants suppose. The court is not required to give effect to a legislative "decree" or "edict," unless every enactment by the law-making power of a State is to be so characterized.

It is not declared that every establishment is to be deemed a common nuisance, because it may have been maintained prior to the passage of the statute as a place for manufacturing intoxicating liquors. The statute is prospective in its operation—that is, it does not put the brand of a common nuisance upon any place, unless, after its passage, that place is kept and maintained for purposes declared by the Legislature to be injurious to the community. Nor is the court required to adjudge any place to be a common nuisance simply because it is charged by the State to be such. It must first find it to be of that character—that is, must ascertain, in some legal mode, whether, since the statute was passed, the place in question has been, or is being so used, as would make it a common nuisance.

Equally tenable is the proposition that proceedings in equity for the purposes indicated in the thirteenth section of the statute are inconsistent with due process of law.

" In regard to public nuisances," Mr. Justice Story says, "the jurisdiction of courts of equity seems to be of a very ancient date, and has been distinctly traced back to the reign of Queen Elizabeth. The jurisdiction is applicable not only to public nuisances, strictly so called, but also to purprestures upon public rights and property. In case of public nuisances properly so called, an indictment lies to abate them, and to punish the offenders. But an information also lies in equity to redress the grievance by way of injunction." 2 Story's Eq., sections 921, 922.

The ground of this jurisdiction in cases of purpresture, as well as of public nuisances, is the ability of courts of equity to give a more speedy, effectual, and permanent remedy than can be had at law. They can not only prevent nuisances that are threatened, and before irreparable mischief ensues, but arrest or abate those in progress, and by perpetual injunction, protect the public against them in the future; whereas courts of law can only reach existing nuisances, leaving future acts to be the subject of new prosecutions or proceedings. This is a salutary jurisdiction, especially where a nuisance affects the health, morals or safety of the community. Though not frequently exercised, the power undoubtedly exists in courts of equity thus to protect the public against injury: District Attorney *v.* Lynn and Boston R. R. Co., 16 Gray, 245; Att'y Gen'l *v.* N. J. Railroad, 3 Green's Ch. 139; Att'y General *v.* Tudor Ice Co., 104 Mass. 244; State *v.* Mayor, 5 Porter (Ala.), 279, 294; Hoole *v.* Att'y General, 22 Ala. 194; Att'y General *v.* Hunter, 1 Dev. Eq. 13; Att'y Gen'l *v.* Forbes, 2 Mylne & Craig, 123, 129, 133; Att'y Gen'l *v.* Great Northern Railway Co., 1 Dr. & Sm. 161; Eden on Injunctions, 259; Kerr on Injunctions (2d Ed.), 168.

As to the objection that the statute makes no provision for a jury trial in cases like this one, it is sufficient to say that such a mode of trial is not required in suits in equity brought to enjoin a public nuisance. The statutory direction that an injunction issue at the commencement of the action is not to be constructed as dispensing with such preliminary proof as is necessary to authorize an injunction pending the suit. The court is not to issue an injunction simply because one is asked, or because the charge is made that a common nuisance is maintained in violation of law. The statute leaves the court at liberty to give effect to the principle that an injunction will not be granted to restrain a nuisance, except upon clear and satisfactory evidence that one exists. Here the fact to be ascertained was, not whether a place, kept and maintained for the purposes forbidden by the statute, was, *per se*, a nuisance—that fact being conclusively determined by the statute itself—but whether the place in question was so kept and maintained. If the proof upon that point is not full or sufficient, the court can refuse an injunction, or postpone action until the State first obtains the verdict of a jury in her favor.

In this case, it cannot be denied that the defendants kept and maintained a place that is within the statutory definition of a common nuisance. Their petition for the removal of the cause from the State court, and their answer to the bill, admitted every fact necessary to maintain this suit, if the statute under which it was brought was constitutional.

Touching the provision that in prosecutions, by indictment or otherwise, the State need not, in the first instance, prove that the defendant has the permit required by the the statute, we may remark that, if it has any application to a proceeding like this, it does not deprive him of the presumption that he is innocent of any violation of law. It is only a declaration that when the State has proved that the place described is kept and maintained for the manufacture or sale of intoxicating liquors—such manufacture or sale being unlawful except for specified purposes, and then only under a permit—the prosecution need not prove a negative, namely, that the defendant has not the required license or permit. If the defendant has such license or permit, he can easily produce it, and thus overthrow the *prima facie* case established by the State.

A portion of the argument in behalf of the defendants is to the effect that the statutes of Kansas forbid the manufacture of intoxicating liquors to be exported, or to be carried to other States, and upon that ground are repugnant to the clause of the Constitution of the United States giving Congress power to regulate commerce with foreign nations and among the several States. We need only say, upon this point, that there is no intimation in the record that the beer which the respective defendants manufactured was intended to be carried out of the State or to foreign countries. And, without expressing an opinion as to whether such facts would have constituted a good defence, we observe that it will be time enough to decide a case of that character when it shall come before us.

For the reasons stated, we are of opinion that the judgments of the Supreme Court of Kansas have not denied to Mugler, the plaintiff in error, any right, privilege, or immunity secured to him by the Constitution of the United States, and its judgment, in each case, is accordingly affirmed,

We are, also, of opinion that the Circuit Court of the United States erred in dismissing the bill of the State against Ziebold & Hagelin. The decree in that case is reversed and the cause remanded, with directions to enter a decree granting to the State such relief as the Act of March 7, 1885, authorizes

It is so ordered.

NOTE B.

POLICE STATISTICS FOR FIFTY-EIGHT AMERICAN CITIES.

Cities.	License Fee for ordinary Saloons.	Number Licensed Saloons.	Population, 1887.	Number Population to One Saloon.	Total number Arrests in 1886.	No. Arrests for Drunkenness, Disor. Con. and Assault.	Number Arrests for Drunkenness.	No. Population to One Arrest for Drunkenness.	No. of Population to One Arrest.	Per Cent. of Arrests for Dr'nkenness, Dis. Con., etc., to Total
Little Rock........	$1,000 00	47	25,877	550	2,013	900	493	53	13	48
Hannibal...........	850 00	35	16,502	471	641	641	227	63	20	100
Austin.............	600 00	52	23,000	443	1,252	971	421	55	18	78
Bloomington.......	600 00	52	22,000	423	909	558	311	71	24	61
Rockford..........	600 00	24	19,500	812	352	247	169	116	55	70
St. Louis..........	550 00	1,600	500,000	375	19,031	9,305	3,247	154	26	48
Brockton..........	501 00	18	20,783	154	950	775	681	31	22	81
Aurora............	500 00	37	19,000	514	428	292	203	93	44	69
Chicago...........	500 00	3,760	800,000	212	40,998	25,407	*24,407	......	20	62
Peoria.............	500 00	150	33,000	220	2,618	957	560	59	13	36
Quincy............	500 00	103	34,500	335	869	505	202	171	39	65
Springfield (Ill.)...	500 00	112	30,000	268	3,002	1,027	512	59	99	34
Wheeling..........	450 00	130	32,000	246	1,409	*1,000	336	95	23	71
Boston.............	375 00	2,695	390,406	145	23,129	19,835	13,304	29	17	66
Chelsea............	350 00	30	25,709	857	1,197	816	714	36	21	68
Grand Rapids......	‘0 50	150	50,000	306	1,415	948	708	71	35	67
Detroit............	.00 00	1,026	‡33,209	130	6,845	5,850	4,101	32	19	85
East Saginaw......	300 00	187	29,141	155	1,520	797	549	53	19	52
Haverhill..........	300 00	84	21,795	259	794	585	489	45	29	76
Lowell............	300 00	430	64,051	149	3,393	2,504	2,260	29	19	73
Saginaw...........	300 00	62	13,207	232	540	212	138	99	25	40
Waltham..........	300 00	8	14,609	1,824	467	305	270	54	31	65
Holyoke...........	225 00	132	27,894	232	1,223	949	687	124	23	77
Covington.........	200 00	180	35,000	104	1,098	901	343	102	32	82
Hartford..........	200 ‘0	300	45,000	150	......	3,051	1,861	24	......	......
New Britain.......	200 00	106	17,000	160	457	344	148	115	35	75
New Haven........	200 00	350	70,000	200	5,802	4,273	3,122	22	12	73
New London.......	200 00	59	12,000	203	892	609	449	24	13	72
Newport (Ky.)....	200 00	‡18	20,500	173	736	522	90	227	28	71
Norwich...........	200 00	90	15,112	168	796	556	383	39	19	70
Racine.............	200 00	96	19,636	204	211	211	146	134	93	100
Savannah..........	200 00	225	45,000	200	1,968	1,068	490	100	23	54
Waterbury.........	200 00	194	26,000	134	1,587	917	610	42	16	58
Fall River.........	190 00	358	58,863	164	2,367	1,997	1,455	40	20	84
New Albany (Ind.).	150 00	62	20,000	322	......	128	95	210	......	......
New Bedford.......	150 00	63	33,393	530	1,151	945	807	41	30	82
Ogdensburg (N. Y.).	150 00	41	11,000	268	†200	†224	90	122	42	84
Buffalo............	125 00	1,926	225 000	168	9,544	5,324	2,803	80	22	56
Evansville.........	125 00	78	40,000	533	1,884	863	385	104	21	45
Lafayette	125 00	236	21,000	89	751	227	188	112	28	30
Wilmington........	100 00	211	42,478	201	2,057	1,315	638	65	20	64
Yonkers...........	100 00	136	20,000	147	940	624	383	52	21	66
Poughkeepsie	95 00	82	20,207	246	445	230	174	615	45	53
Binghampton	75 00	141	22,361	158	972	782	566	39	23	80
Brooklyn..........	75 00	3,080	‡800,000	266	25,709	16,582	12,044	66	31	66
New York.........	75 00	9,199	1,350,000	147	73,928	31,237	18,198	147	19	42
Paterson..........	75 00	600	§70,000	116	2,088	1,974	827	84	25	74
Baltimore..........	50 75	2,250	365,000	162	27,200	20,649	8,247	45	14	76
Allentown.........	50 00	24	25,000	1,042	345	216	112	223	72	63
Cumberland.......	50 00	75	12,000	160	481	423	392	31	25	88
Jersey City........	50 00	1,056	153,513	146	5,894	4,287	1,572	82	26	72
Memphis..........	50 00	200	60,000	300	6,263	2,253	1,074	56	10	35
Orange............	50 00	94	15,231	162	848	547	354	43	18	64
Syracuse...........	50 00	530	77,000	145	3,785	2,304	1,609	48	20	61
Cohoes............	40 00	155	21,426	145	601	404	144	149	35	67
Albany............	30 00	893	96,336	105	4,460	2,610	1,867	52	21	59
Hoboken..........	27 00	338	37,721	112	1,840	1,305	566	66	20	71
Scranton..........	20 00	100	65,000	650	1,245	972	914	71	52	78
Total............		34,514	5,315,777		304,279	217,560				

* For drunkenness and disorderly conduct.   † For nine months only.   ‡ Based on official estimates of one year ago.   § Based on increase from 1870 to 1880.

NOTE C.

The following is the process by which can be computed the number of persons in each of the four classes "temperate drinkers," "careless drinkers," "free drinkers," and "habitually intemperate," in England and Wales.

We know the total number of deaths of males over 25 years to be, by the official reports, 261,066.

We know also the number of deaths of males over 25 years of age in each class to have been (approximately) 101,430, 69,111, 40,163, and 40,263 respectively. If we had the rate of mortality in each class, it would be a simple thing, of course, to compute from the number of deaths the number of the living. But we have only the *comparative* rate of mortality from the report of the British Medical Association, as follows:

TABLE IX. AVERAGE AGE AT DEATH FOR EACH CLASS.

Class A.. 51.22 years.
" AB.. 56.72 "
" B.. 62.13 "
" BC.. 62.42 "
" C.. 59.67 "
" CD.. 60.35 "
" D.. 57.59 "
" DE.. 53.64 "
" E.. 52.03 "
Unclassified... 60.91 "

In this table classes A, B, C, D, and E represent respectively the total abstainers, the temperate drinkers, the careless drinkers, the free drinkers, and the habitually intemperate. When there was doubt in which of two classes to place the death, it was referred to one of the subordinate classes AB, BC, CD, or DE. For instance, if there was doubt whether the man belonged to Class B or Class C he was put in Class BC. The number of deaths in each of these classes was as follows:

Class A.. 122 deaths.
" AB.. 54 "
" B.. 1529 "
" BC.. 178 "
" C.. 977 "
" CD.. 112 "
" D.. 547 "
" DE.. 100 "
" E.. 603 "
Unclassified... 12 "

      Total.. 4234 "

Counting one-half the cases in Class DE as belonging to Class E, we obtain the average age at death for this class as follows:

$$50 \times 53.64 = 2,682.00$$
$$603 \times 52.03 = 31,374.09$$
$$653 \times 52.15 = 34,056.09$$

This gives us 52.15 years as the average age at death for the 653 cases in E and half DE. To obtain the age for all the classes outside E and one-half DE we have the following figures:

$$122 \times 51.22 = 6,248.84$$
$$54 \times 56.72 = 3,062.88$$
$$1529 \times 62.13 = 94,996.77$$
$$178 \times 62.42 = 11,110.76$$
$$922 \times 59.67 = 58,297.59$$
$$112 \times 60.35 = 6,759.20$$
$$547 \times 57.59 = 31,501.73$$
$$50 \times 53.64 = 2,682.00$$
$$12 \times 60.91 = 730.92$$

$$3581 \times 60.15 = 215,390.69$$

This gives us, as the average age at death of persons outside Class E, 60.15 years, and those in Class E, 52.15 years. As the comparison began at the 25th year, we find that those in Class E live, on an average, 27.15 years beyond that point, and those ouside Class E, 35.15 years, or 8 years longer.

Let X = number living in all classes except Class E.
Let y = yearly death-rate for all " " " "
As the number of males over 25 years of age is about 21.5 per cent. of total population, 32,250 will be the number of males over 25 years in a population of 150,000.
$32{,}250 - X$ = number living in Class E.
$y + 8 \cdot 35\, y$ = yearly death-rate " " "
$X\, y$ = one third of 3581, = 1194
$(y + 8 \cdot 35\, y)\, (32{,}250 - X) = 217$; from which we get
$y = .0424$, death-rate outside Class E.
$X = 28{,}160$, number persons " " "
$y + 8 \cdot 35\, y = .052+$ death-rate in Class E.
$3225 - X = 4090$, number persons " " "
If in a population of 150,000 there are 4,090 habitual intemperate drinkers, in a population of 27,870,586 the number of such persons will be 759,922.

Computing in the same manner the number of persons in Class D (including one-half CD and one-half DE) we find it to be 4,865 in a population of 150,000 or, in the entire Nation, 903,917.

APPENDIX. 221

NOTE D.

COMMITMENTS TO JAIL FOR CRIME IN CONNECTICUT.

Compiled from Official Returns and Jail Records, by E. P. Augur, Middletown, Conn.

Year	Number of Commitments	Mod. Drinkers and "Habitually Intemperate."	Drunkenness and Com. Drunkards.	Ass'lt, A. and B. and Breach of Peace.	Resisting Officers.	As'lt with Intent to Kill, Murder and Manslaughter.	Theft or Larceny	Vagrancy	Setting Fires or Arson	Burglary	Violating Liquor Law	
1852												Agitation for repeal of Maine Liquor Law, begun in 1867.
1853												
1854	1,116		541	179	1	3	137	17	10	41	94	"MAINE LAW."—PROHIBITION.
1855	1,248		600	204	1	7	128	14	10	36	116	
1856	1,387		478	318	3	11	256	9	13	25	28	
1857	1,897		664	451	2	11	301	29	14	73	13	
1858	1,787		617	471	0	19	372	85	14	35	14	
1859	1,793		738	419	1	14	332	43	8	34	8	
1860	1,825		763	391		27	346	45	5	62	18	
1861	2,009		672	457		9	331	1	6	71	15	
1862	1,518		493	325		7	190	5	10	35	1	
1863	1,568		515	243		13	282	12	8	25		
1864	1,193		331	202		6	166	13	3	42	1	
1865	1,583		379	245	16	17	386	52	5	50	1	
1866	1,827		537	273	8	50	440	67	12	64	4	
1867	1,693	—	444	275	−16	−49	325	−63	−6	−96	−1	
1868	1,821		575	280	15	31	375	75	14	71	2	
1869	2,246	1,992	842	428	28	85	382	62	9	101	7	
1870	2,593	2,370	1,050	202	52	40	408	97	6	66	8	
1871	2,805	2,658	1,290	339	31	61	387	110	6	78	5	
1872	2,985	2,718	1,470	447	−38	−31	315	164	−8	−60	−27	Sept. 15.
1873	4,481	4,086	2,125	594	63	29	582	170	13	103	14	License, September 15. Law took Effect September 15, 1872.
1874	4,418	3,712	2,044	661	73	45	564	214	19	117	19	LICENSE LAW.
1875	4,425	4,294	2,175	734	52	38	498	235	9	132	24	
1876†	3,103	2,894	1,317	391	34	30	284	149	19	85	†10	
1877	4,149	*2,928	1,734	571	49	28	428	193	24	158	17	
1878	4,577	4,458	2,141	572	60	43	513	279	12	172	14	
1879‡	3,834	3,701	1,628	496	‡43	41	373	221	‡13	125	‡34	
1880	4,142	*3,934	1,827	584	46	24	423	160	12	136	33	
1881	4,332	*4,089	2,226	517	100	48	252	140	8	124	25	
1882	4,825	*4,656	2,612	606	87	41	375	202	17	107	19	
1883	5,394	4,797	2,747	937	93	31	433	266	10	159	13	
1884	5,806	5,678	2,879	961	100	53	460	368	9	151	23	

†1876, eight months, April 1 to December 1.
‡Tramp Law went into effect.
*Returns incomplete on this head.

NOTE E.

GOVERNOR MARTIN'S LETTER.

On the 12th of July, 1887, Governor Martin, of Kansas, sent to the Associated Press the following letter:

WILLIAM HENRY SMITH, General Manager Associated Press: *My Dear Sir*—On the 2d of July instant a special dispatch was sent from St. Joseph, Mo., to a Chicago paper, in which it was stated that "the closing of the saloons in Atchison, Kan., has cut off the most profitable source of revenue, amounting to thousands of dollars a year, and, as a result, the city has not revenue to keep going; that the police force, with the exception of the Marshal and one policeman, had been suspended: that the services of the firemen were to be dispensed with, and that the gas and electric lights were to be shut off."

This dispatch was utilized by the Associated Press, and thus published in all parts of the country. As a result, I have received many letters from different sections making inquiry as to the truth of statements it embodied, and have seen its alleged facts commented on in dozens of newspapers, as evidence that the abolition of saloons has reduced a prosperous city in Kansas to the verge of bankruptcy. Similar letters have been received by the Mayor of Atchison, and by many other cities of Kansas.

The dispatch referred to was prompted by two motives. It was first sent from a town in Missouri for the purpose of injuring a rival city in Kansas; and second, it was inspired by the whisky interest, and intended to create the impression that an efficient city government could not be maintained without the revenue derived from liquor licenses. The city of Atchison has been for many years one of the most important railroad and commercial centres of Kansas. It has a population of about 23,000 people. If the whisky interest could create the impression that Achison had been materially injured because the saloons had been driven out of it, a serious blow would be dealt the temperance cause. The Associated Press, in giving this false special such wide publicity, was made the unconscious agent of a malicious slanderer, whose purposes were as unworthy as his statements unfounded. I deem it my duty to correct the false impressions thus created, and respectfully ask that this letter be given as wide a publication as the dispatch which prompts it.

I am thoroughly familiar with the condition of the city of Atchison, and personally know that the statements embodied in the St. Joseph dispatch are false and misleading. The gas, electric lights, and water supply of the city have never been turned off. Its fire department has been and is continuously on duty. Its police force has been largely reduced, but has, in the absence of the saloons, been ample to preserve the peace and protect the property of its citizens. A local dispute concerning methods of taxation and involving the adoption of a tax which has been collected in the city of St. Joseph for many years past, is the only foundation for the malicious and untruthful dispatch from that place.

Atchison abolished the last of its saloons in the fall of 1886. The whisky interests prophesied that this action would seriously injure the business of the city. It has had no such effect. Atchison is more prosperous to-day than it has been for many years past. Its wholesale trade aggregated over $40,000,000 in 1886, and during the first six months of 1887 this trade increased fully 33 per cent. over that for the corresponding six months of 1886. All the principal streets of the city are now being paved.

More substantial improvements are being made and more buildings are being erected in Atchison this year than during any previous year in its history. Ten important lines of railway centre in the city, and the Southern Kansas Railway has just extended its line to Atchison. The central shops of the Missouri Pacific road have recently been located there; the largest lumber yard in the West has recently been established there, and many other important commercial and manufacturing industries have been located there during the past six months. Better than all, too, hundreds of thousands of dollars that were formerly wasted in the saloons are now expended in feeding and clothing and housing the people, and as a result housands of wives and children in Atchison who were living in poverty a few years ago are now prosperous, happy and contented.

This St. Soseph dispatch is only a fair specimen of hundreds of false and malicious statements I have seen published in the newspapers of the country during the past three or four years concerning Kansas and Kansas towns. The whisky interests predicted that the abolition of saloons in Kansas would injuriously affect the material prosperity of the State, and falsehoods, intended to confirm this view, are constantly invented and circulated in every section of the country, and especially in States where movements are being made to banish the saloons. I am receiving letters daily from different States, making inquiries concerning the effects and results of our temperance laws on the financial, commercial and other material interests of our State, and these letters all indicate that the work of maligning Kansas is going on in every section of the country. Permit me, therefore, to give you the real facts.

The Prohibition Amendment to our Constitution was adopted in the autumn of 1880, and the first laws to enforce it went into effect in May, 1881. The war to banish the saloons was for some years only partially successful. The Amendment had been adopted by a very meagre majority, and the public sentiment in all our larger cities was overwhelmingly against it. As late as January, 1885, saloons were open in fully thirty of the larger cities of Kansas, including Topeka, the capital of the State.

But steadily and surely the public sentiment against them spread and intensified. The small majority that had voted for the Amendment was reinforced first by those law-respecting citizens who are always willing to subordinate their personal opinions to the majesty of law, and second, by an equally large number, who, observing the practical results following the abolition of saloons in different cities and towns, became convinced that Kansas would be a more prosperous, happy, and in all respects a better community of people if it had not an open saloon within its borders. So the sentiment of Kansas against the liquor traffic has grown and strengthened until to-day I very much doubt whether, of its 300,000 male voters, more than 75,000 would, if they could, invite back and reinstate the saloon.

One argument of the whisky interest, viz., that saloons promote the prosperity and growth of communities, has been answered in Kansas by the convincing logic of facts. In 1880 the population of this State, as shown by the census, was 996,096; in March, 1886, as shown by the State census, it was 1,406,738. and it is now fully 1,650,000. In 1880 Kansas had only 3,104 miles of railroads within her borders; on the 1st of March last the State Board of Railroad Assessors reported 6,208 miles for taxation, and from 600 to 800 miles will be added to this aggregate before the close of the year. In 1880 the assessed value of all real and personal property of the State aggregated only $160,891,689; on the 1st of March, 1886, the total was, $277,575,363; and for the present fiscal year the returns thus far received indicate a total of $300,000,000. In 1880 there were 5,315 schoolhouses, 2,914 churches and 347 newspapers in Kansas; there are now fully 6,500 schoolhouses, 3,500 churches and 700 newspapers. In 1880 only 55 towns and cities had populations in excess of 1,000 each; in 1887 more than 200 towns have each over 1000 inhabitants; fully 25 have each over 5,000, and 4 have each over 20,000. In 1880 only 8,868,000 acres were planted in crops; this year the area planted exceeds 16,000,000 acres. In 1880 the values of the farm products of Kansas was only $84,521,000; for 1886 their value was over $264,000,000. For the fiscal year 1880 the percentage of State taxation was 5 1-2 mills; for the present fiscal year the total percentage levied for all State purposes is only 4 1-2 mills.

During the past two years and a half I have organized seventeen counties in the western section of the State, and census-takers have been appointed for four other counties, leaving only two counties remaining to be organized. The cities and towns of Kansas, with hardly an exception, have kept pace in growth and prosperity with this marvellous development of the State. Many of them have doubled their population during the past year. And it is a remarkable fact that several cities and towns languished or stood still until they abolished their saloons, and from that date to the present time their growth and prosperity has equalled, and in some instances surpassed, that of other places with equal natural advantages.

Summing up, the facts of the census confute and confound those who assert that the material prosperity of any community is promoted by the presence of saloons. So far as Kansas and all her cities and towns are concerned, the reverse of this assertion is true. The most wonderful era of prosperity, of material, moral and intellectual development, of growth in country, cities and towns, ever witnessed on the American Continent has been illustrated in Kansas during the six years since the temperance amendment to our Constitution was adopted, and especially during the past two years, the period of its most energetic and complete enforcement.

Yours very respectfully, JOHN A. MARTIN.

NOTE F.

The "Bowman decision" of the United States Supreme Court was rendered March 19, 1888. Briefly stated, the facts in the case were as follows. George A. Bowman and Fred. W. Bowman were brewers doing business in Marshalltown, Iowa. May 20, 1886, they offered 5000 barrels of beer to the Chicago & Northwestern Railway Co., for transportation from Chicago to Marshalltown. The railway refused to transport the beer because of a clause in the Iowa law forbidding all lines of transportation to bring beer into the State unless a permit has been given by the auditor of the county to which the beer was destined. The Bowman Bros. brought suit for damages against the railway. The United States Circuit Court for the Northern District of Illinois decided in favor of the defendant. The case was appealed to the United States Supreme Court, which reversed the decision of the Circuit Court and found for the plaintiffs on the ground that this section of the Iowa law was unconstitutional. Following is the decision in part:

"It is conceded, as we have already shown, that for the purposes of its policy a State has legislative control, exclusive of Congress, within its territory of all persons, things and transactions of strictly internal concern. For the purpose of protecting its people against the evils of intemperance it has the right to prohibit the manufacture within its limits of intoxicating liquors; it may also prohibit all domestic commerce in them between its own inhabitants, whether the articles are introduced from other States or from foreign countries; it may punish those who sell them in violation of its laws; it may adopt any measures tending, even indirectly and remotely, to make the policy effective until it passes the line of power delegated to Congress under the Constitution. It cannot, without the consent of Congress, expressed or implied, regulate commerce between its people and those of the other States of the Union in order to effect its end, however desirable such a regulation might be.

"The statute of Iowa under consideration falls within this prohibition. It is not an inspection law; it is not a quarantine or sanitary law. It is essentially a regulation of commerce among the States within any definition heretofore given to that term, or which can be given; and although its motive and purpose are to perfect the policy of the State of Iowa in protecting its citizens against the evils of intemperance, it is none the less on that account a regulation of commerce. If it had extended its provisions so as to prohibit the introduction into the State from foreign countries of all importations of intoxicating liquors produced abroad, no one would doubt the nature of the provision as a regulation of foreign commerce. Its nature is not changed by its application to commerce among the States.

"Can it be supposed that by omitting any express declarations on the subject Congress has intended to submit to the several States the decision of the question in each locality of what shall and what shall not be articles of traffic in the inter-State commerce of the country? If so it has left to each State, according to its own caprice and arbitrary will to discriminate for or against every article grown, produced, manufactured or sold in any State and sought to be introduced as an article of commerce into any other. If the State of Iowa may prohibit the importation of intoxicating liquors from all other States it may also include tobacco, or any other article, the use or abuse of which it may deem deleterious. It may not choose even to be governed by considerations growing out of the health, comfort, or peace of the community. Its policy may be directed to other ends. It may choose to establish a system directed to the promotion and benefit of its own agriculture, manufactures or arts of any description, and prevent the introduction and sale within its limits of any or of all articles that it may select as coming into competition with those which it seeks to protect. The police power of the State would extend to such cases, as well as to those in which it was sought to legislate in behalf of the health, peace, and morals of the people. In view of the commercial anarchy and confusion that would result from the diverse exertions of power by the several States of the Union, it cannot be supposed that the Constitution or Congress have intended to limit the freedom of commercial intercourse among the people of the several States. * * * *

"It may be said, however, that the right of the State to restrict or prohibit sales of intoxicating liquor within its limits, conceded to exist as a part of its police power, implies the right to prohibit its importation, because the latter is necessary to the effectual exercise of the former. The argument is that a prohibition of the sale cannot be made effective, except by preventing the introduction of the subject of the sale; that if its entrance into the State is permitted, the traffic in it cannot be suppressed. But the right to prohibit sales, so far as conceded to the States, arises only after the act of transportation has terminated, because the sales which the State may forbid are of things within its jurisdiction. Its power over them does not begin to operate until they are brought within the territorial limits which circumscribe it. It might be very convenient and useful in the execution of the policy of Prohibition within the State to extend the powers of the State beyond its territorial limits. But such extra-territorial powers cannot be assumed upon such an implication. On the contrary, the nature of the case contradicts their existence. For if they belong to one State, they belong to all, and cannot be exercised severally and independently. The attempt would necessarily produce that conflict and confusion which it was the very purpose of the Constitution by its delegations of national power to prevent.

"It is easier to think that the right of importation from abroad and of transportation from one State to another includes, by necessary implication, the right of the importer to sell in unbroken packages at the place where the transit terminates for the very purpose and motive of that branch of commerce which consists in transportation, is that other and consequent act of commerce which consists in the sale and exchange of the commodities transported. Such indeed was the point decided in the case of *Brown* v. *Maryland*, 12 Wheat. 419, as to foreign commerce, with the express statement, in the opinion of Chief-Justice Marshall, that the conclusion would be the same in a case of commerce among the States. But it is not necessary now to express any opinion upon the point, because that question does not arise in the present case. The precise line which divides the transaction, so far as it belongs to foreign or inter-State commerce, from the internal and domestic commerce of the State, we are not now called upon to delineate. It is enough to say, that the power to regulate or forbid the sale of a commodity, after it has been brought into the State, does not carry with it the right and power to prevent its introduction by transportation from another State."

Three Justices, Waite, Harlan, and Gray, filed a dissenting opinion.

www.ingramcontent.com/pod-product-compliance
Lightning Source LLC
Chambersburg PA
CBHW020812230426
43666CB00007B/979